Embracing Rough-and-Tumble Play

Embracing Rough-and-Tumble Play

Teaching with the Body in Mind

Mike Huber, MAEd

Photographs by Angelia Sampson

Redleaf Press®
www.redleafpress.org
800-423-8309

Published by Redleaf Press
10 Yorkton Court
St. Paul, MN 55117
www.redleafpress.org

First edition 2017
Cover design by Jim Handrigan, with photo color and retouching by Tim Meegan
Cover photograph by Angelia Sampson
Interior design by Mayfly Design
Typeset in the Whitman and EPF typefaces
All photos by Angelia Sampson except by Chris Bonhoff on pages 28, 87, 110, 131, 136, 170, 171 (top left; bottom); and by Mike Huber on pages 1 (right), 12 (lower), 27 (right), 34, 44, 47, 48, 54, 62 (left), 64, 65, 70 (right), 72, 74, 75 (right), 97, 99, 100, 104, 113, 118 (left), 119, 128, 140, 141, 143, 145 (left), 159 (left), 160 (top), 161 (top left), 164 (bottom), 173, 175 (bottom).

Printed in the United States of America
24 23 22 21 20 19 18 17   1 2 3 4 5 6 7 8

Library of Congress Cataloging-in-Publication Data
Names: Huber, Mike (Early childhood educator)
Title: Embracing rough-and-tumble play : teaching with the body in mind /
  Mike Huber ; photographs by Angelia Sampson ; additional photographs by
  Chris Bonhoff and Mike Huber.
Description: St. Paul, MN : Redleaf Press, 2016. | Includes bibliographical
  references and index.
Identifiers: LCCN 2016013405 (print) | LCCN 2016014758 (ebook) | ISBN
  9781605544687 (pbk.) | ISBN 9781605544694 (ebook)
Subjects: LCSH: Movement education.
Classification: LCC GV452 .H83 2016 (print) | LCC GV452 (ebook) | DDC
  372.86—dc23
LC record available at http://lccn.loc.gov/2016013405

Printed on acid-free paper

For the Twin Cities big body play discussion group:
Becky, Damian, Joey, Joshua, Ross, and Tom

Contents

6 Environment with the Body in Mind 129

Acknowledgments

I want to thank Tom Bedard, Joshua Koeppe, Joey Schoen, Ross Thompson, Damian Johnson, and Becky Klay for our monthly discussion group. Our conversations about big body play, rough-and-tumble play, and risk were the basis for this book. I also want to thank Angelia Sampson, who took most of the photographs in the book. Fifteen years after being her preschool teacher, I was able to collaborate with her on this project. It was amazing to see what a truly gifted artist she has become. I am grateful to the programs that let Angelia and me photograph them in action: Jalilia at Training Up a Child, Joseph and Lori at For the Children Child Care, Kristenza and David at Dodge Nature Preschool, and Maureen's Day Care. I could not have written this book without the advice of Naomi Siegal, Nancy Boler, Julie Nelson, and Gill Connell. And finally, I am indebted to Sara Wise for shaping my ideas into this book.

Introduction

We were moving. I was an enlightened teacher. I knew children needed to move as part of their healthy development. It was morning group time, and I was having the children move to music. We were making up a story about lions waking up and running and leaping. All the children were moving and contributing ideas. Well, almost everyone. Greg had ducked behind a shelf. I tried to get him involved, but he said he was tired. I gently tried a few more times but didn't want to pressure him. Maybe next time I can get him moving, I thought.

Soon I had the lions wash their paws for snack. Greg waited until the others were done and washed his own hands. As we finished snack and got ready for freeplay, Greg told me he was going to "attack the bad guys." Suddenly, this quiet child put on a cape and held a wand up high and pretended to shoot at all the bad guys. He leaped to his right, ducked behind the couch, rolled on the ground, and stuck his wand out again. A few other boys joined him. Sometimes they attacked the bad guys. Sometimes they jumped and rolled on each other. It was as if something inside Greg had woken up, something that I was unable to wake up. I thought I was an enlightened teacher, but I realized I knew nothing.

Why I Wrote This Book

I am exaggerating, of course, but the thing about teaching is that just when you think you know what you are doing, you realize there is more to learn. I knew children need to move, but I didn't always recognize it. The truth is, a few years ago I would have told Greg and the other boys to calm down when they started roughhousing, the very thing that got them moving (and for Greg, the only thing). Planning movement activities is not enough. Getting children outside for long periods of time is not enough. Even having a mat set aside for boisterous, rough-and-tumble play is not enough. Children need a sense of power, a chance to take risks, and a choice in how they move their bodies throughout the day. Greg and many others like him do need to move their bodies, but they might not do it when the teacher plans it. We can't address a child's physical development for fifteen minutes and then the child's literacy skills the next fifteen minutes. We need to be aware of the whole child the whole day.

How My Teaching Changed

I started teaching young children twenty-three years ago. I learned from some great teachers. I observed and tried to get to know each child as an individual. I learned to give kids hands-on experiences and use open-ended conversations. Things went well for more than fifteen years until one year when I had a classroom with eight boys and two girls (with just me as the teacher). The eight boys were active and fairly typical boys. This is when I discovered how the techniques I learned from classes and from mentors were geared toward behaviors more typical of girls. It was a very stressful year, and it was the first time I honestly considered leaving the classroom.

Meanwhile I was training other teachers about gunplay and warplay. I wanted others to see how children can learn from this type of play. Participants at my workshops often asked about rough-and-tumble play, and I was quite limited in my knowledge. I decided to do some research. I went to a workshop by Michelle Tannock, an expert on rough-and-tumble play. As she spoke, I couldn't help thinking about my own childhood. Somehow I had put behind much of what I did as a child when I learned about expectations for group care. I often wrestled with my older brother and sister. I often jumped on the couch, rolled on the cushions, and ran into walls just for the sheer joy of it. Why didn't I allow the children in my care to do the same? I started my research to create a workshop for other teachers. Little did I know how much my own teaching would change.

As I learned more about the need for children to move, I started to change my expectations in the classroom. Movement isn't one time in the schedule. It is a constant need. It is more than the vigorous activity that children engage in. It is also the squirming and fidgeting that happens during calmer activities. The children are more aware of the need than we are as teachers. This awareness of the body is the beginning of what some might call mindfulness, an awareness of the present.

Some of the changes I made happened quickly, usually the Monday after a good workshop or after reading a book. Other things happened gradually over time. Five years later, I had another class with eight boys and two girls, and I had a great time. I seemed to be able to keep all the children engaged and keep my own sanity.

Over those five years, I presented my workshop "Boisterous Boys (and Girls)" to hundreds of early childhood educators. This was a topic that many were ready for. I learned a lot from providers who had come up with techniques or activities for active children. They didn't necessarily know the research, but they knew what worked for them. I learned as much from these people, most of them women and most of them family child care providers, as they did from me. I also learned from people who worked in child care centers and school-based preschool programs. All of these people affected my own teaching practice. This book brings together many ideas that have improved my teaching and helped me better appreciate the loudest, most active kids in my classroom.

The Body and Mind Connection

We don't teach children how to be curious. They are curious by nature. As teachers, we try to pique their curiosity to draw them in and engage them. Other times, we simply encourage their curiosity. More than anything, we try not to squelch that curiosity.

The same should be true for movement. Children are born to move, and they move almost constantly. This repetition gradually makes movement automatic. Until basic movements are automated, children use much of their brainpower for motion rather than cognitive functions (Connell and McCarthy 2014). We don't need to teach kids how to move, but we do need kids to move if we are to teach them.

Children should be allowed to use their bodies to express themselves throughout their time in early childhood programs. I think this includes allowing children to have more freedom in how they choose to sit or stand for activities.

I think children should also choose whom they play with and what they play. That is not to say that we shouldn't set limits, but we need to rethink what many of those limits are in a typical classroom. Limits should foster our expectations for the whole child. We, as teachers, shouldn't get too focused on one developmental goal at a time. Children will be learning many things simultaneously, and they will remember things that involve multiple stimuli. We also need to make sure that our goal for children is not simply obedience.

This means making quite a few changes from some typical teaching practices. I hope this book can help you and others make some of the changes without making as many of the mistakes I made along the way. Of course, you will make mistakes also, but that means you are moving out of your comfort zone. Throughout the book, I've provided background information about why some changes make sense. I offer stories from my own classroom (and a few other classrooms as well) to bring the information to life. I have included step-by-step guides for things that I have found to be stumbling blocks for teachers; for example, "I understand that kids should do woodworking, but I don't know anything about tools" or "I'm willing to let kids roughhouse, but I've never done anything like that before."

Allowing young children more freedom of movement with their bodies will benefit everyone. Active children, especially boys, will be more successful, and teachers will spend less time managing behavior. I think many teachers will have less stress around boisterous behaviors. And finally, all children learn more when they are moving (even if they are just shifting sitting positions), although some will have to move more than others.

Who Is a Teacher?

In this book, I use the term *teacher*. Not everyone involved in the education and care of young children uses the term. I use the term *teacher* to refer to anyone teaching a child or children. I am mostly thinking of early childhood education professionals (such as family care providers, center-based child care providers, out-of-school-time providers, therapists, and administrators), as well as self-defined "teachers." It could also apply to a parent, a grandparent, an uncle, an aunt, an older child, a younger child, or anyone who interacts with young children.

The teacher could be in any type of program: family child care, after-school care, tutoring, child care center, preschool, nursery school, religious education, school-based pre-K, kindergarten, or early elementary classrooms. In chapter 6, I focus on interest areas more commonly found in a full-day child care center or family child care program. I do this because I feel that these programs have the biggest number of interest areas. Other types of programs may only have a few interest areas. My intent is not to ignore these other types of programs but to allow each of you to take what you need from the book. For example, if you are teaching Sunday school at a church and don't have a block area, you can skip over that section.

One word of warning: I want to caution elementary school classroom teachers not to think that this book does not pertain to you. It is true that children are more able to delay gratification as they get older. However, the expectation that children can control the impulse to move their bodies until one short recess in the middle of the day is fraught with peril. I think more research has to be done to determine the impact of having six-, seven- and even eight-year-olds sit for a

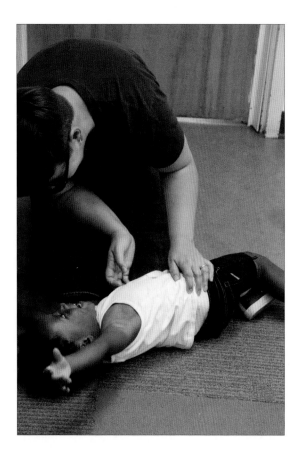

majority of their school day. We have accepted this as the norm while at the same time we have seen a significant rise in obesity and diagnoses of ADHD. Some research shows that "exercise improves learning on three levels: first it optimizes your mindset to improve alertness, attention, and motivation; second, it prepares and encourages nerve cells to bind to one another, which is the cellular basis for logging in new information; and third, it spurs the development of new nerve cells from stem cells in the hippocampus" (Ratey 2008, 53). In the meantime, it falls on those who work in after-school and other out-of-school-time programs to get kids moving more.

I will go out on a limb and add that some kids need full-body contact, such as running into a pile of cushions or mat on a wall. I think allowing the children who need this type of contact five minutes in the morning and five minutes in the afternoon (in addition to recess) would allow the teacher to spend less time disciplining the same child. I don't think this is any different than taking a child out of the room for fifteen minutes for speech or other types of therapy.

All Children

This book is written for teachers working with all children. Obviously children vary in physical abilities and interests. You may need to adapt some of the activities or suggestions for individual children. My hope is that we get all children moving more. For example, children in wheelchairs may not be able to run, but they can wheel around. The book does not cover specific adaptations because adaptations will vary greatly depending on the needs of the children you are working with.

This book is also for children regardless of gender. All children need rough-and-tumble play and freedom of movement. Therefore I will use the terms *child* and *children* unless the gender of the child is important to the situation. I will also use gender-neutral pronouns (*they* and *them*) when referring to a child if the gender is not known or I am referring to any child.

Having said that, I believe the implications of this book will directly impact boys the most, particularly preschool boys who tend to have a testosterone spike around the age of four. Rough-and-tumble play, for example, is a favorite way for many boys to play. This type of play is seldom encouraged—and often discouraged—currently in early childhood education and out-of-school-time programs. Meanwhile boys are referred for special needs and expelled from preschool at a much higher rate than girls (Froschl and Sprung 2008; Gilliam 2005). (See chapter 1 for more discussion on gender.)

No matter the gender of the children in your care, they all need to move more for the sake of healthy development and learning. Children express themselves physically as often as they do verbally. As teachers, we need to see them for who they are. I hope this book helps you find ways to support children in their full expression. Feel free to skip around the book to find the information that will work best for you.

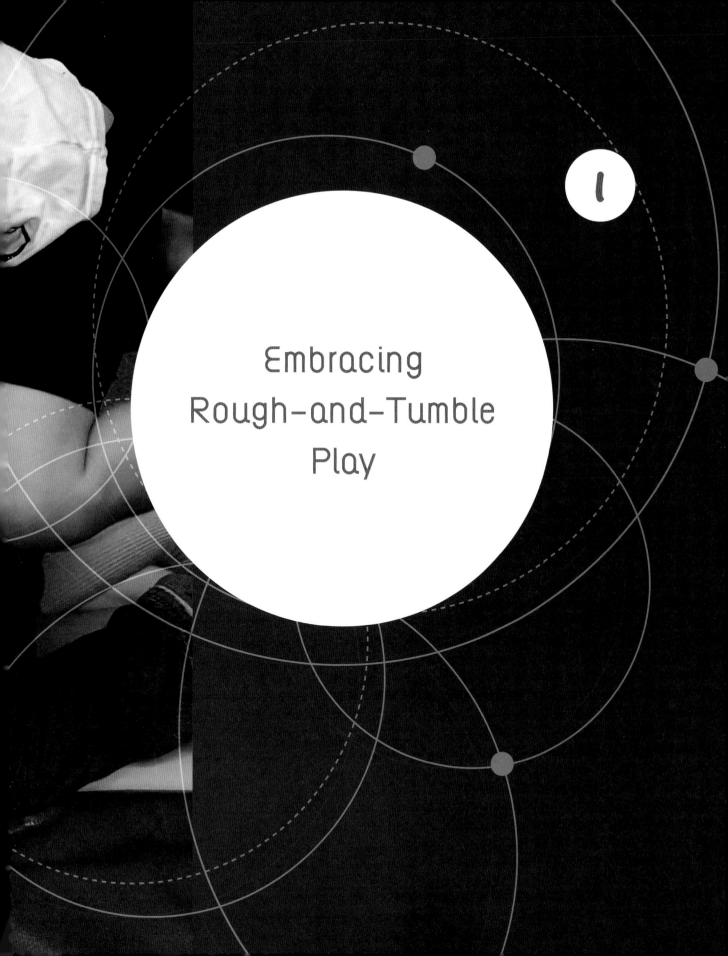

Embracing Rough-and-Tumble Play

mbracing rough-and-tumble play? Isn't that the type of play I try to *stop* from happening in my classroom? I spent years gently reminding children that we don't play that way inside. I often talked about teaching the whole child, meeting their needs in all learning domains: social-emotional, literacy, cognitive, and physical development. But looking back, I ignored many of the children's needs for physical development by telling them to wait until we were outside. I was failing to see a vital part of who these children were.

Rough-and-tumble play, play that involves the whole body, whether it is running, spinning, falling, or roughhousing, is the purest form of what it means to be a child. It is the two-year-old jumping up and down, waving their arms up and down, yelling, "Mommy! Mommy!" at the end of a day at school. It is the four-year-old spinning and falling and then getting up and spinning again. It is the time when children are so engrossed in the joys of movement that they lose all track of time. As we grow into adulthood, we see this same total immersion of the mind and body when a dancer executes a phrase with extreme focus and precision, or when a surgeon completes a complex procedure and saves a life. Sometimes this immersion in movement is as simple as tending to a garden or rocking a child to sleep.

I embrace rough-and-tumble play because it is literally a type of embrace. It is a way for children to show affection for another while also testing the limits of their own physical abilities. Children need tender affection, such as cuddling and hugs, but children also need to be physical in a more vigorous way. Both types of contact can strengthen social bonds.

I also embrace children's boundless energy and their need to move almost constantly. Movement is the basis for all exploration and expression. Children explore who they are and what they are capable of while also exploring the world around them. Children express themselves through movement and sound to communicate with those around them.

In the past few decades, the field of early childhood education has undervalued movement in general, especially rough-and-tumble play. We seem to expect three- and four-year-olds to sit without fidgeting or squirming, expectations that were once reserved for elementary school students. Meanwhile elementary school students often go to after-school programs where they are expected to sit after a full day of sitting in classes. This mistrust of movement has affected regulatory agencies that focus on safety at the expense of wellness that children achieve through physical play. Higher education has also failed to emphasize the importance of movement for all learning when training our future teachers. We need systemic change in the various state licensing regulations and in the education of future teachers of young children if we are to allow children to become active learners.

Terminology: Rough-and-Tumble, Big Body Play, and Body in Mind

Rough-and-tumble play is often misunderstood. People often immediately think of a classroom in complete chaos with children knocking one another over. It is important to remember that it is play, not fighting; it is fun for all those involved. Psychologist Harry Harlow used the term *rough-and-tumble play* to describe the play of rhesus monkeys in the 1950s (DeBenedet and Cohen 2010). He observed and described how they chased one another and grabbed, pushed, and tumbled. This type of play is all around us. You can see dogs do the same thing.

Research has been slowly building on rough-and-tumble play. The research has shown that there are many benefits from rough-and-tumble play in terms of cognitive, social, and physical development (DeBenedet and Cohen 2010).

One time I was with a class of toddlers at the zoo. I was bringing two of the children back to the bus. The path followed the edge of the wolf pen. As we approached, a wolf was standing just on the other side of the fence. The toddlers were face-to-face with the wolf. Their eyes seemed to meet. The toddlers smiled. The wolf ran away, but two or three strides in, it stopped and looked at the children. They knew what to do. They ran after the wolf. The wolf would run, but every few steps it would slow down until the toddlers were just a few feet away, and then it would run. When it reached the other end of the path, the wolf waited until the toddlers caught up and then ran back the other way. The children and the wolf clearly knew how to play chase without uttering a word. Looking back, I realize that it also started with the children and the wolf looking at one another's faces to signal that a game was happening.

The term *rough-and-tumble play* has come to include all play using the full body, including body contact with another individual; body contact with objects; and striking objects with feet, hands, or an object, such as a racket or bat. This definition even includes running, climbing, and other (possibly) solitary activities (Tannock 2011). In other words, much of play labeled *rough-and-tumble* is neither rough nor does it involve tumbling.

In 2011 Frances Carlson introduced the term *big body play* with her book of the same name, *Big Body Play: Why Boisterous, Vigorous, and Very Physical Play Is Essential to Children's Development and Learning*. The term essentially covers the same type of play as rough-and-tumble play with a few additions of more solitary play, such as stomping and spinning. It also describes these full-body activities more accurately. This type of play involves the whole body. Sometimes it is rough, and other times it is not, but it is always "boisterous" and "vigorous." Many teachers find

that parents and administrators are more recep-
tive to the term *big body play* rather than
rough-and-tumble play. While I don't expect
everyone reading this book to allow roughhousing in the classroom, I think most teachers can
find ways to include more climbing, pillow
fights, and stomping in their daily routine (for a
more complete picture of big body play, see
chapter 5).

I have chosen to use the term *the body in
mind* to include behaviors that aren't necessarily play, such as sitting in various ways or moving through a classroom in various ways. The
term also implies that the body and mind are
not easily separated. We are always teaching a
whole child, but too often we forget that we
don't have distinct times to teach the body and
other times to teach the mind. All domains are
developing simultaneously. We may focus on
one domain, but children are the amalgamation
of their physical, social, emotional, creative,
and cognitive developments.

If we think of movement as a facet of child development in the same way we
think of literacy development, perhaps more of us will allow children to express
themselves with their bodies throughout the day. I don't think any teacher would
tell a child to wait to talk to a friend because it wasn't literacy time, and yet we
try to restrict children's bodies most of the day. Not only is physical development
an important part of a child's development, it is an integral part of all the other
domains. The human brain works based on input from the body through the
senses, but it is always dependent on motor skills to help the body interact with
the world.

While children should have freedom of movement as much as possible, there
are obviously times when their choices are limited. For example, they need to sit
in a car with a seat belt or car seat. They should also have a calm body while eating to reduce the risk of choking. Adults may need to set these limits and others
for safety reasons.

One other important thing adults can do to keep children safe is to let children know that they get to decide who touches them. Children can decide if they

want a hug or not. A child will need to be touched if they are unable to care for themselves, such as diapering, but the adult should verbally let the child know what they are doing. There may also be times when a teacher needs to prevent a child from hitting another child, but again, they should say something like, "I can't let you hurt others." Otherwise, children should be taught to speak up when they don't want to hug or to sit on someone's lap. Also, children should be taught what constitutes abusive touch and how to tell someone about it.

Adults can also keep children safe in this regard by having clear policies and procedures. While abuse of young children by teachers is "exceedingly rare" (Carlson 2006), all staff should be screened for a history of sexual or violent records before hire. Allowing big body play may involve more touch between children and adults, but exercising the above strategies will not only keep this play safe but will teach children valuable lessons that they can build on as they get older.

Gender: The Elephant in the Room

Any discussion of physical play and active children needs to address the concept of gender, but I have purposely avoided making this book about boys for a number of reasons. I think that all children have to use their whole bodies in a variety of ways. Studies have shown that all children engage in big body play as well (Tannock 2011). On the other hand, I must acknowledge that boys tend to

engage in big body play significantly more often, and some boys can be significantly more boisterous in relation to the other children (Tannock 2011). This is especially true when you look at big body play involving contact: one study found that four-year-old boys were seven times as likely to engage in this type of play as other types of play. Interestingly, the same study found that three-year-old boys were only twice as likely to engage in contact play (Smith and Connolly 1972).

I also avoided making a book about boys because I want to encourage teachers to look at each child as an individual. When we look at large numbers of children, we can make broad statements, such as "boys tend to" or "girls tend to," but when we look at an individual child, we can only comment on what we see that particular child do. Gender is tendency, not destiny. Of course each child does a range of things. There is a range of activity level, noise level. Play can be collaborative or solitary. When we start putting certain behaviors in a blue box or a pink box, we can miss this range. Girls *do* engage in rough-and-tumble play, and they *do* engage in warplay. Boys *do* play family, and they *do* sit and draw. My fear is that if we start putting different types of play in different boxes, we may not notice the things that don't fit in those boxes—or worse, the people who don't fit in those boxes. There are boys who are not okay with physical contact, and there are girls who enjoy it. And yes, there are children who are perceived to be boys, but who may not have come to their full gender identity as a girl (or vice versa).

Kay woke up and put on her black pants with the skulls. She wore her blue sneakers and her Ninja Turtles sweatshirt. Some days she would put on a white sweater, a pink skirt, and patent leather Mary Janes. Every night she had a dream that would tell her if she was supposed to be a boy or a girl that day. Then she would know what to wear and which lunch box to bring. She always used the pronouns *she*, *her*, and *hers*, and she would often say, "I'm a girl that dresses like a boy," but other times she would say, "I'm a boy today."

Did she play differently when she was dressed as a boy than when she was dressed as a girl? The truth was that Kay behaved the same way whether dressed in black or pink, whether she expressed herself in feminine or masculine ways. She liked to play family. She would get out dishes and have a birthday party for the baby. She also liked to wrestle on the mat or play superhero.

Kay tries to express her gender in very concrete ways with her clothing and lunch box just like most four-year-olds. However, when it comes to play, her play doesn't fit easily into gendered categories. We often think of superheroes and rough-and-tumble as ways that boys play, but there are plenty of girls who play these games, and there are some boys who don't. It is easy to categorize some types of play as inherently "boy" or "girl" play, but I think it's more realistic to think of play as a continuum. A continuum allows for more variation. Meanwhile a child may be able to slide from one end to the other (and back).

The continuum could also be based on noise level or activity level. It could be based on fantasy play that emphasizes nurturance ("family") or protection ("good guy vs. bad guy"). It could even be thought of as masculine and feminine (or boy and girl). The difference is that each child can slide back and forth on a continuum rather than be boxed in to certain expectations.

Each individual's spectrum will look different. There are boys who seldom engage in such rough-and-tumble play, and there are girls who engage in it frequently. There are also children who may be identified by adults as boys due to their biological sex but who self-identify their gender as girls, as well as those who do not identify as boys or girls or who identify their gender differently than their biological sex. My fear is that as soon as we start labeling certain teaching strategies as boy strategies or girl strategies, we might lose sight of the fact that most strategies work for a majority of children. In a review of several studies on gender and play, sociologist Barrie Thorne (1993, 104) found that "within-gender variation is greater than the differences between boys and girls taken as groups." One study found 15–20 percent of boys scoring high on a measure for rough-and-tumble play, but 80–85 percent of boys and girls were indistinguishable. Too often researchers focus on the 15–20 percent and make generalizations about an entire gender (Thorne 1993). One study even found little difference between boys and girls in terms of rough-and-tumble play patterns (Jones 1972). Children must be appreciated for who they are.

At the same time, there are studies that show that when boys are inactive, their brains can lapse into a neural rest state and shut down by as much as 70 percent (Morhard 2013). I am not sure if we would find this true of all boys. For that matter, I am sure we could find girls who also tune out when they are inactive. Regardless, all children's brains are more active when their bodies are active.

Boy "Culture"

It is helpful to think of this tendency among boys to engage in rough play and to move around as a culture. Not all boys exhibit the expressions of "boy culture," and some girls and gender-nonconforming children do. Whether or not certain actions are cultural versus biological is beyond the scope of this book. I am merely focusing on the teachers' responses to this type of behavior, especially if that teacher isn't part of this "boy culture."

I also think that there is a culture within the field of early childhood education that comes from having an almost exclusive female workforce. While there is a wide array of variations within this culture, there is a tendency to favor sitting and reading books over other narrative media (e.g., storytelling, acting, or video). There is often a rejection of certain types of play, such as violent-themed play and roughhousing, that is common among boys. The result is a culture clash.

None of this is intentional. Many of these teachers may not have needed to move as much as many of the boys (and some girls) in their classrooms. Teachers are unknowingly using their cultural expectations to determine what is acceptable.

The benefit of looking at this as a culture clash is that it makes the difference visible so that teachers can build a bridge between cultures. We commonly make an effort to respect

and accommodate cultural difference in our classrooms. For example, if a child in your classroom is a Jehovah's Witness and therefore doesn't celebrate birthdays, you wouldn't make a birthday crown for them even if you make one for others. You would hopefully talk to the family and do your own research to find out what else you can do to help that child feel comfortable. You wouldn't change your own cultural attitude toward birthdays, but you would likely accommodate cultural differences.

We can apply the same concept to teachers who may not have grown up with the need to move around while listening to someone read a book. You don't need to understand the impulse, you simply need to be aware that the impulse exists in others. You should be aware that this impulse exists in girls as well. I find that teachers often allow boys more latitude than girls in terms of physical play. We all need to make a conscious effort to support the play that children engage in regardless of gender.

Following the ideas in this book and observing the children in our care through the lens of celebrating full body expression will help teachers find ways to appreciate all children. Teachers can learn other ways of supervising and working with children. For many it will be a bit like learning a foreign language. It starts by understanding a little bit. Gradually you learn more. Although you may never learn all of it or speak it like a native, you will still be able to serve the needs of the children who do in a culturally responsive way.

Native Speakers in Charge

As I have said, research shows that boys engage in rough-and-tumble play much more often than girls. When I talk to most teachers, I often hear that girls seldom engage in this type of play. However, when I talk to teachers (both men and women) who allow and encourage rough-and-tumble play, I get a very different picture. These teachers all agree that big body play or rough-and-tumble play seems fairly mixed gender-wise. For example, I have eight boys and two girls in my preschool class this year, but about half the time when someone asks me to get out the mats for roughhousing, it is a girl. When kids are piled on top of one another, there are girls and boys in the mix.

I have found that girls are more likely to engage in rough-and-tumble play when I do. I also find that all kids participate in activities that the adults around them clearly love. If a teacher loves painting and is very enthusiastic while taking

out some paint, many children will come over and paint. It makes sense to me that if a teacher has fun roughhousing, most kids will participate, regardless of gender. I think that as more teachers accept big body play, researchers will see more girls engaging in it.

In either case, all children need to engage in vigorous physical play at least sometimes. While all teachers can adapt to include more of this play, children could benefit from more male teachers in the classroom because men tend to have grown up with more physical play. I think one of the reasons there are so few men in the field is the lack of big body play. In a survey of members from the National Association for the Education of Young Children about male teachers, several members responded that there are few male teachers because they lack nurturing skills. As one respondent put it, "Men have not had as much experience with nurturing, discipline, bonding traditionally" (Nelson 2002, 17). Of course, some men are nurturing (and some women are not). More importantly, men nurture "in ways that are different than women," such as big body play (Nelson 2002, 28). It is not uncommon for men who try teaching in early childhood settings to feel judged by other teachers and parents when they start playing rough with children.

Duke was one of the fathers at the child care center where I was working. Duke was unemployed at the time our cook left. Our director offered him the job. Duke gladly accepted, and we were soon enjoying the lunches he cooked as well as his visits to the classrooms. The kids loved having him visit, and Duke clearly loved being there.

After a few weeks, the director asked if he wanted to substitute for one of the aides in the afternoon. Soon he was subbing a few times a week in one of the classrooms. He became the only African American male teacher at the center. Our classrooms were fairly typical of the time. There was a block area with plenty of blocks, a dress-up area with lots of costumes, several choices of toys, and lots of art supplies. But when Duke was in the classroom, most kids forgot about all our precious materials. They wanted to play with Duke.

Duke offered the children something I and the other teachers did not. Duke loved to roughhouse. If he was in the room, he usually had one kid in his arms (often upside down) with two or three kids grabbing his legs, and everyone shrieking in delight.

I hate to admit it, but the other teachers and I often asked Duke to tone it down. At best, we tolerated Duke's roughhousing, but we certainly didn't try to emulate or even learn from him.

Looking back, I can see that Duke was giving the children something they desperately needed. If we start encouraging these interactions, we may see more male teachers.

Implications for Fathers and African American Families

Going a bit further with this analogy of "culture," fathers are usually native speakers in terms of big body play. This may be a good way to get fathers involved. You must first create a culture where big body play is accepted in your program. As you do this, more fathers may feel comfortable in the classroom or program. You can also ask fathers to visit. Ask them if they would like to read a book, play chase, or maybe both. Don't assume they have to play physically, but let them know it is an option. I find that many families allow roughhousing at home, and many fathers are involved in this play, but these same families often have the perception that rough-and-tumble play is looked down on by teachers. You need to be proactive by letting them know you appreciate this type of play.

Head Start studies have found that fathers are much more likely to get involved if the program makes an effort to include fathers and if "the father believes his participation can make a difference" (Head Start Bureau 2004, 9). This is particularly important because, culturally, many people consider the care of young children to be the mother's job, and on top of that, many fathers have negative associations with school based on their own experiences when they were younger. If we are to make fathers feel welcome, the first step is to show them that we want their children in our programs.

African American families should be a primary focus for this change in our schools. The fact is that "African-Americans attending state-funded prekindergarten were about twice as likely to be expelled as Latino and Caucasian children, and over five times as likely to be expelled as Asian-American children" (Gilliam 2005, 3). On top of that, "many young [African American] boys have a deep fear of authority figures such as policemen—and this fear can extend to teachers" (Morhard 2013, 73). All of

us need to make sure we are building trusting relationships with all the children in our care, but we also need to be clear that collectively we are failing to do this with many African American children.

The study on expulsions identifies behavior problems as the main reason. It also found that if there was a classroom-based behavior consultant, the expulsion rate went down significantly. I think if teachers offer children more outlets for physical play and movement throughout the day, there will be fewer behavior problems and thus fewer expulsions. It is not the children who are at fault: it is our expectations. On top of that, boisterous behavior may be read differently when the child is an African American boy. What may be considered typical rowdy behavior for most children may be misinterpreted as aggression for African Americans. This creates a cycle in which the mistrust the child may have is met with more vigorous discipline, creating even more mistrust. The statistics are so dire that it is urgent we find ways to break this cycle.

Child Readiness

For more than a decade, many in the early childhood education field have focused on school readiness. At its best, school readiness was intended to help teachers focus on facilitating development for all children in all learning domains. At its worst, school readiness has encouraged too many teachers to focus on literacy and math skills because that is what schools test. Even worse, within these developmental domains, children are "taught" using methods once reserved for first or second graders. Literacy is based on speaking, listening, and nonverbal language. Children naturally practice this when they play and have meaningful conversations. Written language is learned much more effectively with a foundation in verbal and body language. Math skills as well are based on experiences building and playing with toys and other objects. Marginalizing play means marginalizing real learning for many children.

I am not opposed to children being ready for school, but I want to focus on helping them build the foundation to be lifelong learners. This requires children to be able to move and interact with others much more freely than we often allow, and it requires me to be very intentional about my teaching. Direct instruction is important but is reserved for the things children can't discover on their own.

I hope more teachers will focus on the child readiness of schools rather than the school readiness of children. We need to ask ourselves, is our school ready for children to move their bodies as much as they should? Is our school ready to support children with the social skills they have and help them develop more skills? Is our school ready to give children the time, space, and materials they need to explore and discover?

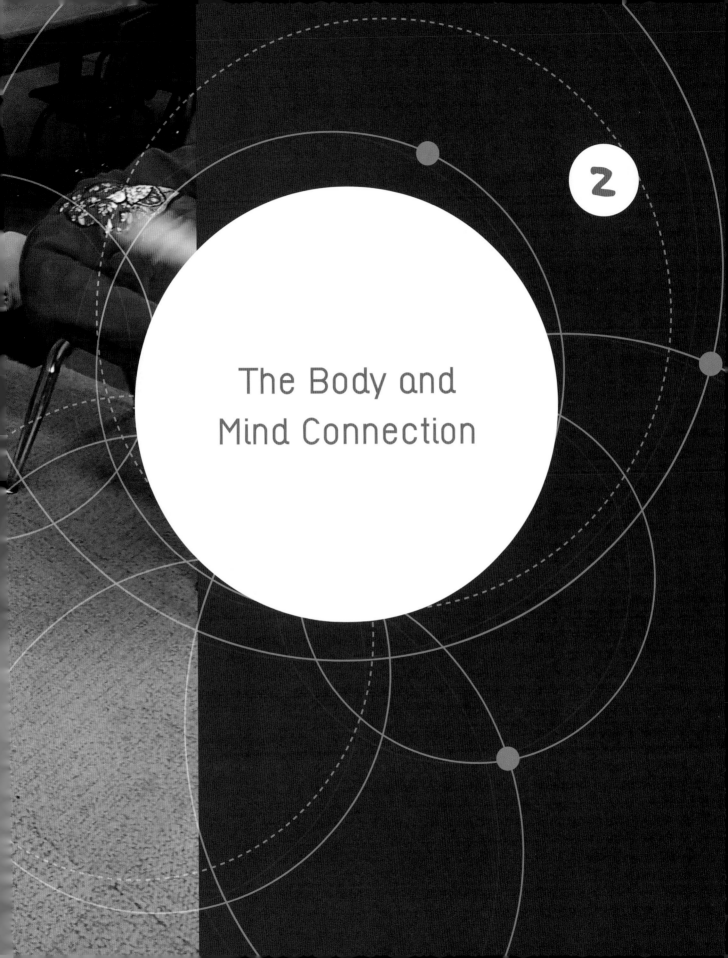

The Body and Mind Connection

2

It all starts with movement. Even before we were born, we were rocked in the womb by the movement of our mothers. We were born through the movement of our mothers and our own reflexes working together to enter into the world. We all were born with reflexes necessary for our survival. As our brain developed, reflexes gave way to intentional movement. These movements allow us to explore and express ourselves. Exploration leads to cognitive development as we make sense of the world around us. Expression becomes creative expression through the arts as well as language, both written and oral, as we try to communicate with others. The body and mind are completely interdependent.

We can see how this body and mind connection works by looking at motor development and how it progresses through early childhood. Then we can look at how motor development influences other developmental domains. In this chapter, I focus on social-emotional development. I also touch on literacy and cognitive development and how it relates to movement.

Motor Development

"Children learn about the world by moving. They need all sorts of experience moving their body through space, manipulating objects to learn about firmness, pressure, and force." This is how Naomi Siegal (pers. comm.), an occupational therapist, describes how children learn. In order for children to develop physically, they need to move their bodies almost constantly. But it's not just physical development that happens through movement. Before you can learn to read or write, certain basic movements need to be automated so that you don't have to concentrate on staying in your chair or keeping the book in your hands while tracking the print with your eyes. Most math concepts are first learned by manipulating objects, building with blocks, putting materials together and taking them apart. In fact, all learning has some physical component involved—either through movement or the senses.

This physical learning continues throughout our lives, but in the early years it is the foundation on which all future learning is built. Somehow we have forgotten this as a society. I believe that children under the age of eight should be moving their bodies more often than sitting still during their waking hours. Most of us wouldn't think of stopping a baby from trying to pull themselves up to standing because we know that is how the baby will learn to stand and walk. But we often stop toddlers, preschoolers, and first and second graders from moving because we are busy "teaching" them. All children need to be moving.

When we talk about physical development, we often break it down into gross-motor and fine-motor skills. I think this misses the bigger picture. What is really happening is that children are developing muscle control from the trunk and gradually mastering muscles further out on their limbs. Infants and toddlers have much more control of their upper arms than their fingers, for example.

When a preschooler starts using a pincer grasp to hold a pencil, they are showing fine-motor coordination, but that grasp also requires them to anchor the rest of their body in a way that facilitates drawing or writing. The gross-motor skills are still necessary, but many of them will become automatic for the child. Fine-motor skills develop in the context of gross-motor skills (Connell and McCarthy 2014).

This is important because we are trying to help children learn dexterity for a vast number of actions. If children only had to learn to write, we could have them imitate the pincer grasp as toddlers, and eventually they could probably do it. However, they would have a tougher time also using their hands to brush their teeth, thread a needle, type on a keyboard, or play a piano. As teachers we need to help children experience movement so those actions can become automatic and they can continuously become more precise in their movements.

Gill Connell and Cheryl McCarthy (2014) refer to motor development as developing power, control, and coordination. Children focus mostly on power as they develop skills, at first using too little or too much power. Gradually they gain control over their movements individually, and finally they coordinate their movements with other movements and sensory input. Of course all of these are always happening simultaneously, but the focus shifts as children get older. While children tend to develop in the same sequence, the timing will be different for each child. Some children won't develop in a typical way. I will talk about typical behavior, but you must observe the children in your care to see where they are developmentally. If you have concerns or think a child has special needs, consult with parents as well as a developmental pediatrician or other health practitioner.

Infant Motor Development: Building a Strong Foundation

Infants learn mostly by using their five senses as well as their vestibular sense. The vestibular sense includes balance, alertness, concentration, and posture.

Infants move their limbs and head as they gradually gain more control. As they start moving through space, they also begin to develop their proprioceptive sense. The proprioceptive sense includes spatial and body awareness.

Infants' brains and bodies are in an ongoing dance; body movements create information for the brain to process. The brain makes neuron connections based on the stimuli. The brain gains control of the body and directs the body to move based on what it has learned. The body and brain develop together. One doesn't happen without the other.

Infants need uninterrupted time to play and explore with as much freedom as possible. They need to use their muscles to move in the ways they are able. They need to interact with age-appropriate materials, as well as with other children and adults (Post and Hohmann 2011). Infants learn from experiences. Experiences that involve several inputs (e.g., physical, sensory, and emotional) will result in myelination (Connell and McCarthy 2014). Myelination is the brain's way of protecting the axons that connect neurons. Myelination makes the brain work more efficiently and helps retain memories. Myelination is more likely to occur when

infants are free to move about because they are more likely to physically interact with materials and/or people while also involving their senses and emotions. At the same time, they are using the muscles they will need for the next stage in their development.

Adults often have infants strapped in car seats, backpacks, high chairs, and other restrainers. While there are times to use these devices, infants should be able to move their bodies freely as often as possible. Adults also prop infants up with pillows before they are able to sit up themselves. Instead, adults need to let children develop these abilities themselves. Without tummy time, infants' reflexes won't be integrated. If this happens, preschoolers or school-age children need to spend extra time prone to develop these foundational movements to allow for more mature movement (Naomi Siegal, pers. comm.).

Infants can also be active in their own caregiving activities, such as diaper changing. You can encourage them to do parts of the routine themselves, such as moving their legs for you or handing you the diaper. This helps them become aware of their abilities to care for themselves while building trust between the caregiver and child (Post and Hohmann 2011).

Infancy is a time of huge leaps in terms of motor development and brain growth. We don't need to overwhelm them with fancy toys for this to happen. We simply need to provide space, time, and meaningful interactions. They will take care of the rest.

Toddler Motor Development: Always Moving

Toddlers continue to move while building neuron connections in their brains. They continue to learn about the world as well as their bodies and their capabilities. This is the time when they will really challenge themselves to find out what they can and can't do.

Toddlerhood is also when movements become automatic, which means the movement doesn't require conscious thought. This requires them to repeat movements over and over. Anyone watching toddlers understands this. There is no need to tell toddlers to repeat a motion. Rather, adults need to give them time to repeat actions on their own. At first all their attention will be on their actions. As the action becomes automatic, they will be able to talk or otherwise turn their attention elsewhere. Children cannot move onto other types of learning until basic movements are automated.

As mentioned earlier, toddlers are focused on the power in their movements. As they move, they slowly gain in strength, stamina, flexibility, and agility. You cannot circumvent this process. They must complete this stage before developing coordination and ultimately control.

Because toddlers are mostly focused on the power of their movements, there is little subtlety in their play. They run, grab, and crash with abandon. Toddlers can also learn about gentle touches during this time, but they need a focus. Too often we use the phrase "gentle touches" when a toddler is using anything but a gentle touch: pulling the cat's tail, hitting another child, and so on. Toddlers need to hear the phrase "gentle touch" while they are truly using one. This allows them to understand what adults mean by the phrase. As toddlers develop impulse control, they can use a gentle touch with a verbal reminder.

It's a quiet morning in the toddler room. Children are arriving and snuggling with the teacher to read a book. Each child is holding a small cloth doll. Two children are in the teacher's lap, and one is leaning against her arm. Another child is standing facing the teacher. As the monkey in the book calls for its mom, Georgina points at the shelf and says, "Peer . . . peer." The teacher follows her gaze and translates, "Pierce? Is Pierce missing his mommy?" She goes to the shelf and takes Pierce, a toy porcupine, out of his nest. The toddlers gather around, and the more verbal ones offer sympathy. "It okay. Mommy come back." All of them stroke Pierce gently.

The children help Pierce when he misses his mommy. They hug him, stroke him, and cover him in blankets. Younger toddlers occasionally grab him forcefully, but the teacher helps the children use a gentler touch.

Pierce helps the children articulate their own emotions while the teacher can label those emotions. The children can practice their abilities to care for others. Meanwhile they can practice more controlled (gentle) touches.

Preschooler Motor Development: Controlling Movement

Preschoolers are much more able to control their physical movements than toddlers. But they are by no means masters at control and coordination. They still

need plenty of opportunities to move their bodies in big and small ways. However, adults often start to limit movement at this age. Preschool classrooms are often designed to prevent open areas. As any preschool teacher knows, if there is an open area, some children are going to run.

This is unfortunate because these children are still developing a sense of control and coordination. These aren't skills that should wait an hour or two before going outside. They need to practice these skills repeatedly. Of course, preschool classrooms are also full of other materials that are absent in a toddler room. There are more art supplies, block buildings, and structures made from Legos, Magna-Tiles, and other manipulatives. Children need limits, but they can also help decide on the limits based on the guidelines of the classroom (see pages 109–11 on rules and guidelines). This allows the children to assess the situation, see themselves as active participants in their community, and ultimately practice impulse and motor control.

For example, if the kids have decided that a certain spot in the room is safe for running, they need to make sure they are running in that spot rather than near someone's block castle. This requires them to turn or stop without crashing into nearby shelves or walls as the situation warrants. This gives the children opportunity to have movement experiences, as well as practice both movement and impulse control skills. Having a safe place to run also makes my job as a teacher easier. It is much easier to negotiate with children about where it is safe to run than it is to prevent them from running.

Schoolager Motor Development (Ages 6–12): Still Need to Move

Schoolagers are even more advanced in their ability to refrain from big movements for longer periods of time, but that doesn't mean they should. In this book, I focus on early childhood programs as well as out-of-school time (OST) in elementary schools. The logistics of an elementary school differ so greatly that the

topic deserves its own book. However, the need for movement is the same no matter where a child is. As psychiatrist John Ratey puts it in his book *Spark: The Revolutionary New Science of Exercise and the Brain* (2008, 3), "The point of exercise is to build and condition the brain." Our bodies need to be moving in order for our brains to function efficiently and effectively. When we are moving, our body releases a protein called brain-derived neurotrophic factor, which builds and maintains brain cells. Studies show that we can remember things better after exercising (Ratey 2008).

Movement and Social-Emotional Development

Movement is part of motor development, but it influences other developmental domains as well. Emotional development is affected by movement, including self-awareness, self-regulation, and impulse control. Social development also relies on impulse control, including controlling aggression as well as an ability to understand nonverbal communication. None of this development can happen without movement, and the more movement allowed or encouraged for children, the more likely it is that they will experience positive social and emotional development.

Self-Awareness

Impulse control involves a child simultaneously controlling emotions and physical impulses. This starts with body awareness that eventually progresses to

self-awareness, which can be thought of as awareness of one's body and emotions. Any movement can help a child become aware of where their body starts and ends, where it fits in with the surrounding environment, and what their body is capable of.

Big body play in particular helps children become aware of their bodies. They often push themselves to their limits until they have to stop to rest. They breathe heavily, and their hearts beat fast. They can often feel the strain in their leg muscles. This is especially true with roughhousing, where children also become aware of their bodies as they come into contact with other bodies and with the ground. It may seem wild or out of control, but it is very focused in the same way that yoga helps focus attention to one's own body (Nancy Boler, pers. comm.).

In contrast, playing video games results in a spike in adrenaline and an increase in heart rate. However, the body itself is at rest. In this case, there is a disconnect between the body's actions and the body's reaction. Roughhousing is high activity and (some) yoga positions are low activity, but both revolve around an awareness of the body.

This idea of roughhousing as body awareness also gives me deeper appreciation for what the children are doing when they are playing rough. Children learn to decode nonverbal cues and develop and maintain friendships and even take care of one another when they roughhouse (Carlson 2011a; Carlson 2011b).

Children are simultaneously developing body awareness and control of the expression of their emotions. This self-awareness doesn't happen in one continuous upward arc. Every day children are exposed to a variety of sensory input. Children's ability to self-regulate during cycles of high activity and low activity is a big part of social-emotional development.

Self-Regulation

Throughout the day, children go through stages of high activity or high arousal and stages of low activity or low arousal. I often refer to this as amping up and winding down. Most children naturally bring themselves back to a midpoint of stasis. As adults, we don't always give children enough credit for self-regulation (Nancy Boler, pers. comm.). If children exert themselves physically, they will eventually find a time to rest. Some kids will go from one extreme to the other. I have a niece who, when she was three, would ride her tricycle up and down the sidewalk until she literally fell asleep at the wheel. She had to be carried up to bed. Most kids, of course, have a transition between the two extremes.

As a teacher, I have to plan for transitions between high and low arousal. I need to encourage high arousal during the day, but an hour before naptime, I need to help children gradually lower their arousal. I need to make sure that children who are playing actively at this time are showing self-awareness. A child who is playing pillow fight with others and laughing is already showing self-awareness because their attention is on the activity. It will be a matter of gradually lessening the activity level. However, a child who is throwing pillows randomly and shouting seems to be in an excited state and in need of focus. I can't simply lower the activity level for this child because they won't be able to lower their arousal. If I throw a pillow at this child, I am offering myself as a target and focus for the play. I may need to provide more physical contact (hugs, sitting on lap) for this child as we wind down for nap to help the child remain aware of their body. Some children are not able to adjust their arousal state on their own. I need to look for cues to know which children will need my help.

After the pillow fight, we read books. The first book is usually shorter and allows for some child interaction, either with hand motions or joining in on a repeated phrase or rhyme. The next book will usually be a little longer, requiring more mental focus. Then the children use the bathroom and help put out the cots. The activity level winds down slowly so that the children lie down for naptime at least thirty minutes after the pillow fight.

Naptime is the lowest point of activity in our school day, but there are many other smaller cycles of activity. There are days when I wonder if the kids will ever settle down. It is important not to think of high-arousal states as times when they are not focusing or paying attention. Often they are focusing on something. It's just not necessarily what we want them to focus on. Children have to move their bodies around to learn about themselves, or as Connell and McCarthy (2014, 228) put it, "While it may look out of control to us, this self-exploration is actually helping the child learn self-control."

Recently I had an appointment in the morning, so I had a substitute teacher in the classroom for the first two hours of my full-day preschool classroom. When I returned, the volume was quite loud (even for my eight boys and two girls). Ninjas were moving throughout the room. Kids were flying their Lego spaceships complete with sound effects. A few were in front of the CD player engaging in what can only be called full-contact dancing.

I looked around the room. The children seemed focused on their play, but there didn't seem to be room for quiet play if someone was getting overwhelmed. I grabbed some clay from the art shelf and set it on two trays. Soon Frank set down his spaceship and was sitting at the table making "rabbit holes" by pushing his thumb through his lump of clay. He started talking to the assistant teacher about rabbit holes, what he knew about them, and how you make them from clay. She tried making holes with the other lump of clay.

Steve also set down his spaceship also and joined the dancing children. This left the toy area empty. The ninjas soon filled the space. I asked them if they had a safe place to run. Greg, the lead ninja, moved a riser and pushed in a chair and said, "We can run here." Now they were running and hiding on one side of the room while others danced on the other side of the room. I didn't stop anyone from playing boisterously, but I made sure they could see alternatives, and I made sure they had room so they were less likely to interrupt one another's play. An hour later, they had eaten lunch and were sitting quietly while I read books before nap.

There's no use expecting kids to sit quietly if we haven't let them move loudly first.

This story illustrates the need to let children play in a loud, boisterous way so they can cycle into a calmer state as well. Most children are able to do this on their own if we simply let them. Occupational therapist Naomi Siegal says, "All children need to be challenged so they can find their limit and discover ways to recover from stimulus. If they are never challenged, they won't find it" (pers. comm.). The vast majority of children will learn to self-regulate.

Some children may have a hard time winding down. Their behavior may still be very active but less focused, or they may start crying or become physically aggressive. If a child is having a hard time recovering from stimulus, either they need to do heavy work that involves resistance, such as pushing heavy things, or they need gentle and regular movement, such as swinging or rocking (Naomi Siegal, pers. comm.). Some children simply need to have physical contact (see the recovery strategies on the next page). If the problem is ongoing and you have tried several of the above strategies, the child may need to be screened by an occupational therapist.

Nate and I had a good relationship, but he was not what I would call cuddly.

One day Molly was wearing a red cape with a hood. Nate told her he was the Big Bad Wolf. She started to run, and he chased her. My first instinct was to tell him they weren't to run in the classroom. It's not really a rule. We use guidelines, not rules, and the guideline is "We take care of each other." So I watched closely to see if they were taking care of each other.

The two were in control enough that they didn't bump into chairs or tables. Then I noticed something even more impressive. If someone walked in the path they were using, Nate would change paths about ten feet before he reached that person (by this time, Nate had run so far ahead in their circular path that Molly was now chasing him). He did it three different times, so I know it wasn't just a fluke.

They continued this game for about ten minutes, and then Nate stopped at the bookshelf. He grabbed *Little Red Riding Hood* (the book, not Molly) and breathlessly asked me to read to him. I leaned against the cushions in the book area, and Nate rested his head on my arm while I read. We read three more books.

Nate and I did bond while sitting quietly, but he needed to play boisterously first. He didn't have to choose between a quiet activity and a loud one. He needed both.

Recovery Strategies

Heavy Work	Gentle, Repetitive Motions
Push shelving or tables	Swing
Stack chairs	Rock in a rocker or glider
Lift a teacher, push a teacher	Rock on a teacher's lap
Lift a friend	Sway
Carry weighted milk jugs	Roll on an exercise ball or exercise peanut
Push against a wall	

Impulse Control

Self-awareness and self-regulation are important emotional developments, but for children to develop socially, it is arguably most important that they develop impulse control. When children are amping up, it is important that they control their impulses even as they get louder and move their bodies. This can allow them to enjoy their wilder side, and it is easier for them to wind down again when they are ready. Impulse control requires children to respond to stimulus at a similar level. If one child shouts to another child that there is a tornado coming, it is appropriate for that child to shout back, "Let's get out of here!" It wouldn't be appropriate for that child to tackle the first child. The child who tackles is responding to the shouting, not as part of adventurous play, but rather as a personal attack. This would be the "fight" reaction of the fight-flight-or-freeze response to stimulus. It is usually the easiest of the responses to notice as a teacher.

Children may also respond by running away to another part of the classroom or hiding. Often I see the child hiding, but it is difficult to find out why they are upset. I suppose too often I am thinking that someone else must have done something to this child, but just like the child who physically attacked another, this child needs help responding to stimulus.

A child who responds by freezing may stare blankly, often sitting or lying down. It's not always obvious what is going on. If I directly ask a child in this phase what's wrong, I usually don't get a response. Once it happens a few times, it becomes clear that this is their response to loud or active play.

There are things you can do to help children learn impulse control. Games that involve starting and stopping, such as a Freeze Dance, are fun and effective: Children dance to music. When the music stops, they have to stop. Young pre-schoolers often take a few seconds to be able to respond. As they get better at this, you can introduce games like Simon Says, which require a child to listen

to directions but only follow them if the leader says, "Simon says." You can even make it a little harder by playing what I call Backward Bob Says. This game is similar to Simon Says, but instead of following the directions of the leader, you do the opposite. If I say, "Stand up," the children sit down (Galinsky 2010). This requires children to control the impulse of following the direction while simultaneously figuring out what the opposite direction would be (or watching what the other kids do). I find that about half of the four-year-olds in my class can do this consistently.

A much more basic game to encourage impulse control is playing monster or other chase games. You are the monster, and you chase the kids. You make yourself as big and loud as you can. You should start slow with this, not getting too big or too loud until you know what your class can handle. If some children have a fight-flight-or-freeze response, you can gently remind them that it's only a game. If you have children that respond this way, you should not catch them. They should always get away. Once all the children seem to be able to play the game without going into fight-flight-or-freeze mode, then you can start catching them. You should start by catching the kids that seem the most comfortable.

Healing Touch and Tactile Tolerance

Some children may need some extra work with impulse control. I find two tactics work for most of these children: healing touch and tactile tolerance. They both relate to touch, but healing touch is receiving touches from another person, and tactile tolerance is about feeling objects or materials.

Healing touch can be done before boisterous play, even hours before, and still be helpful. This can be especially true for children dealing with stress or trauma. This does not mean they can't engage in physical play, but rather the teacher must be intentional in helping them learn to handle touch. Julie Nelson, an educator who has worked in a therapeutic preschool for decades, says, "The more children have experienced abusive touch, the more they need to experience positive touch" (pers. comm.). That positive touch could be gentle, or it could be part of rough-and-tumble play. At first children in these situations may react negatively and strongly to any touch, but eventually they can learn to tolerate and even enjoy it.

In her book *Essential Touch*, Frances Carlson puts it quite bluntly: "Nurturing touch from their caregivers is essential for children to feel loved and secure." She goes into more detail later in the book:

> When children of any age are denied touch or when they experience it only in the context of aggression or punishment, they are deprived of the nurturing environment they need to thrive and grow. They also will lack experience to prepare them to discern touch that is loving and appropriate from touch that is dangerous and inappropriate. (2006, 3)

The teacher can be proactive by intentionally including healing touch. The idea is to allow the children to have gentle, warm touches without them focusing on the person touching them or trying to read that person's intentions. For example, many children enjoy having their fingernails painted. When a teacher paints nails, they hold the child's hand. Most children tolerate the touch even if they are hyperreactive because they are watching the colors appear on the nails.

Healing touch is used with the intention of helping children who have experienced stress and trauma, but all children can benefit from these activities. However, children should never be forced to participate in any of these activities. The idea is to give them positive experiences with touch. If children are able to tolerate touch, they are much more likely to enjoy roughhousing, superhero play, or other louder, more physical play.

Tactile tolerance activities may also be needed before a child can participate in group activities involving touch (see pages 136–38 for ideas on making a sensory table more inviting for all). If a child still has a hard time dealing with touch after trying these strategies, help from an occupational therapist may be needed. If the child is uncomfortable or stressed by sound, you may want to have the child wear headphones. This can give them a way to participate in activities that

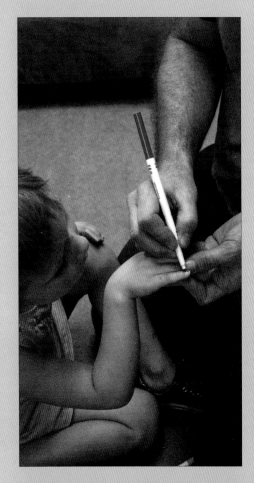

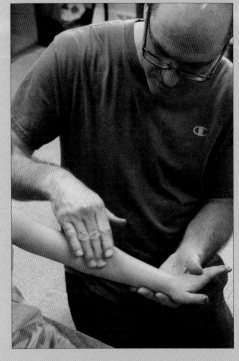

might otherwise be overwhelming. I find that any sound-canceling headphones work, anything with foam covering the ears. They can be ones made for listening to music or ones made specifically to reduce noise (sold in hardware stores).

Healing Touch Strategies

Finger drawing	Being touched on the back is less threatening for most children.	Teacher uses finger to draw letters on a child's back. The child can try to "read" them.
Lotion	Using lotions with a variety of scents (including unscented) and colors.	Teacher's hands stroke child's hands and forearms.
Painting nails	Using watercolor paints, markers, or nail polish to paint child's fingernails.	Teacher gently holds child's hand while painting.
High five	Giving a high five is often a nonthreatening way to initiate some contact with a child.	Teacher holds up hand and asks for a high five. If child resists, the teacher puts own hand down.
Washing up	Some children like to paint their hands and arms. Afterward, they need to wash up.	A teacher can help wash their arms, resulting in similar touch as applying lotion.

Tactile Tolerance Experiences

Soaking feet in soapy water	Fill small tub or dishpan with warm, sudsy water. Have a towel nearby to allow child to dry feet.
Bathing a baby or puppy	Have child wash a doll or stuffed animal in warm, sudsy water. Have towel ready as well as extra clothes.
Using a hair dryer	You can have child use a hair dryer to dry their clothes if they get wet, or just to feel the air.
Hiding pieces in a rice bin	Hide puzzle pieces in a small bin of buckwheat hulls, rice, or beads so child needs to retrieve pieces to finish a puzzle. You can also hide letters needed to complete the alphabet.
Hiding pieces in playdough	Hide beads or other small treasures in playdough for children to pick apart to find.

Aggression

As mentioned above, children who have a hard time regulating their responses to stimulus may become aggressive. Of course all children may become aggressive at times. I have heard from teachers who are wary of allowing roughhousing because some children may not respect the limits of another. Obviously we do not want children to hurt others, but this is the case regardless of whether the play is physical or not. Some children may require more guidance as they learn to roughhouse. Some are easily aroused, and there are some proactive steps you can take before they roughhouse. In either case, these children are exactly the children who should learn how to roughhouse, because it can help them with impulse control and learning to read nonverbal cues. Children who do not show trustworthiness in roughhousing or play in general are socially rejected. It is the role of teachers to help those children earn the trust of others.

Children need body contact with others, but they are not always able to verbalize those needs. Instead, they simply test out contact with others. We can help them learn to articulate their needs and ask others to play with them, but we also have to help them meet the physical need for contact.

Aggression needs to be addressed whether it is relational aggression, verbal aggression, or physical aggression. Roughhousing or other physical play is different from aggression. When children are playing, all players continue to move

Let's Go Wild

Anna and Chris Hahnfeldt, a couple who run Early Bird Day Care out of their home, were worried about Jamie. Jamie was a four-year-old who often jumped on or pushed other kids. The actions seemed random. It was hard for Anna and Chris as well as the kids to predict when it would happen. It was causing some injuries and lots of hurt feelings. It was also resulting in Jamie being shunned by the other children.

Anna and Chris decided that Jamie needed more positive contact with others. They decided to add a new activity. They called it Let's Go Wild. They put down a small mat in the middle of the floor. They had two kids at a time go on their knees on the mat and tumble, tickle, roll, and push each other. While the other kids wait for a turn, they cheer, "Let's go wild!" Anna made a short video to show the parents. When the parents saw the smiles and laughter and sheer excitement of their children, they understood Let's Go Wild time was not something to be worried about but rather something to celebrate.

While all the kids now enjoy Let's Go Wild, Anna and Chris are most pleased with Jamie, who no longer jumps on kids randomly. They found a way for him to meet his need for contact with others. They have also found that there are fewer injuries in their program, and that kids play with Jamie more often.

toward other players, trying to stay engaged in the play. When there is aggression, one child or more is trying to move away from the interaction while the other pursues them. When children are interacting, the teacher can look for the play face from each child. Children put on a "play face" that usually involves a broad smile, raised eyebrows, and accompanied laughing (Brannigan and Humphries 1972), or at the very least, a relaxed, neutral face that indicates nonverbally that they are willing to play. A teacher can also look to see if anyone seems to be trying to get away and listen for sounds of distress or aggression.

There are three types of aggression that children might engage in: relational, verbal, and physical. It is important for teachers to address all of them whether the children are engaging in big body play or any other type of play.

Relational aggression is when a person threatens to discontinue their friendship or tells others not to be friends with that person. Usually this is held as a threat if the victim does not do their bidding. This type of aggression is often overlooked by teachers because it is harder to spot, either because the aggression does not result in a loud conflict or simply because the teacher does not recognize it as aggression (Smith-Bonahue, Smith-Adcock, and Ehrentraut 2015). The teacher can address the feelings behind the child's statement. "You really want them to play with you. You seem worried that they might not play with you." (Or "You seem mad that they don't want to play with you.") Then the teacher can move into conflict resolution, approaching the situation as a problem to be solved.

Early childhood consultant and conflict resolution specialist Betsy Evans (2016) has created a six-step conflict resolution process that I have used for more than fifteen years:

1. Approach calmly, stopping any hurtful actions.
2. Acknowledge children's feelings.
3. Gather information.
4. Restate the problem.
5. Ask for ideas for solutions and choose one together.
6. Be prepared to give follow-up support.

These six steps allow children to identify their feelings, express their concerns, and listen to the viewpoints of others. They not only stop the aggression but help children learn other ways to interact without aggression. I have found that this mediation process works well with verbal and physical aggression as well.

Verbal aggression is when a person threatens or taunts another. I think it is important to address verbal aggression in a way that increases the dialogue rather than shuts it down. Just telling a child to stop talking that way does not allow them to learn from the experience, nor does it allow them to express any issues or concerns they have with the other child in a less hurtful way. Teachers sometimes use the phrase "We do not say that to our friends." This sets up a troubling corollary: Can we say it to someone who is not our friend? Again, I think it is better to use conflict resolution so children can talk about the emotions behind hurtful statements.

Physical aggression is easier to spot. If a child hits another child, that act is usually followed by tears, shouting, or more hitting. It is easy to blame the child who hit first and discipline them. I think it is much more effective to treat the incident as a learning opportunity (Evans 2016; Gartrell 2012). We often don't know whether the child is acting aggressively due to difficulties in regulating emotions and controlling impulses. We also don't know if the child is responding to undetected relational or verbal aggression from the other child (who we often see as the victim). If this is the case, the child may feel victimized by both the child who verbally attacked them as well as by the teacher who has disciplined them. The child may also feel that their feelings have not been acknowledged.

We obviously want to stop any physical aggression, but it should be done as calmly as possible. After that, you can use conflict resolution to stop the current situation and to make future aggression less likely. Some teachers express skepticism, believing that using conflict resolution allows children to hit without repercussions. I have found just the opposite. Since I started using conflict resolution, I have found that children who are physically aggressive usually learn to control their aggression and solve conflicts verbally. This creates a much more peaceful atmosphere where children tend to trust one another.

Nonverbal Communication

Movement and physical play also involve nonverbal communication. Nonverbal communication is an important part of literacy development. In the past, I have often overlooked this. I made sure to have one-on-one conversations with children. I had plenty of group-time experiences where I helped children talk to a whole group. Of course I read with children daily. What I failed to do intentionally was teach kids about the nonverbal aspect of language.

I have always used humor in my teaching, which modeled the importance of tone as well as facial expression. I might scrunch my face up in an exaggerated way and tell the kids, "No having fun." The children know I am joking, because of the absurdity of the statement and also from the relaxed tone (even though I lower the pitch) and the lack of tension in my face, even though I am scrunching it up. It is quite difficult to describe the slight difference in tone or facial expression on the written page. On the other hand, I think the vast majority of people would correctly understand I was joking.

I find that toddlers and preschoolers have a harder time reading body language. I often see toddlers hugging another child who is squirming and pushing away. I see older preschoolers pick up a toy that is right in front of another child even if that child is looking directly at the toy or even reaching for it. The response is almost always, "They weren't using it." The child only noticed the lack

of physical contact—not the other child's gaze (or they were conveniently ignoring it). In the past, I have failed to help children learn to read these cues.

Roughhousing and chase are perfect for teaching how to read body language. Teachers can foster this by articulating what is happening. "He is smiling, so you can keep playing rough," or "She is scrunching her face; she doesn't seem to like it anymore. Let's ask her if she wants you to stop." Some children need more help reading body language. It is important to give them more experience roughhousing even if you have to put some limits on it. You could be the roughhousing partner to start with. Perhaps you will need to use a timer for these children at first when they roughhouse. You can gradually increase the time they roughhouse as they learn to control their impulses and read body language.

Unfortunately, children who don't read body language well are often pulled out of physical activities rather than supported in this play. When a child is learning to read, we don't take books away from the kids who have a harder time reading. The same should be true for the children who have a hard time reading body language. They need more practice with this vital skill, not less.

On the other hand, some kids are very good at reading body language—at least with their friends. I have had to rethink my idea of "using your words" over the last few years as I have included roughhousing. When I first allowed roughhousing, I would tell children to ask before they play rough with someone. But closer observation has caused me to rethink this a bit. It turns out it is much more complicated. Greg and Neville are very close friends. They play together

Neville crashed into Greg. I take a few steps forward. Like a police officer, I am assessing the situation as I approach. Is anyone hurt? Is a fight about to erupt? Is a fight already in progress? Do I need to call for backup? Neville looks up at Greg (he is a full head shorter). Neville is smiling. Greg meets Neville's eyes, and he smiles too. Then Greg tackles Neville to the couch. They erupt into laughter. I look around to see if the area they have chosen is safe for this type of play. They wisely chose the couch. I know that in a few minutes, Neville will cry. It almost always happens that he will get bumped a little too hard. Greg will stop the play and ask if Neville is okay. Neville will cry for about thirty seconds, and Greg will apologize. Then Neville will look at Greg's face and smile. Greg immediately goes into play mode. The two are tackling each other.

It always starts with nonverbal communication. The two know that they are playing. They often tackle each other once or twice before they even talk about what they are playing. After the initial greeting-tackle, one of them will suggest a scenario.

"How about we're superheroes?" "How about we're Ninja Turtles?" "How about we're lions that escaped from the zoo?"

Then play resumes. It is a mixture of verbal and nonverbal communication. If someone winces, the other often eases up. If someone starts laughing, the other will keep repeating the action that led to laughter.

Sometimes they don't even come up with a scenario. They simply enjoy the physical contact.

every day. They frequently play rough together. However, they do not start by asking if they can play rough. They have an understanding.

Greg and Neville have an existing relationship that allows them not to use their words. What about a third child? Greg and Neville often are joined by others who read their body language. If the two of them are rolling on top of each other, another child might also roll on top of one of them. Usually it works. Once in a while, someone will say, "Stop." The other child stops, and trust is built.

If a new child joined our class, I would have to help them join other children who were playing. I find that the most successful way of joining others is *not* to ask, "Can I play too?" The first step is nonverbal. The child (or teacher) needs to play with similar materials. If a child is drawing, draw near them. If they are building with blocks, build near them. In general, anchoring yourself the same way helps as well. If the child already playing is sitting on the floor, the other child should sit. If the child is sitting at a table, the child sits at the table. If the play involves movement, the child entering play needs to move as well. If pretend play is involved, the child should figure out the roles and choose a role to suggest.

Even if the other children don't agree with the role chosen, they will often choose a substitute. "You can't be the mom because we don't have any parents. You can be the big sister." Entering play requires a lot of nonverbal communication first. Similarly, when the child does speak, the tone of voice cannot be too forceful, or even a polite request will go unheeded.

Teachers can play an important role in helping children learn to "read" body language and to express themselves nonverbally. This starts with toddlers.

In general, teachers should help toddlers articulate what they are doing. I think of it as a sports announcer giving a play-by-play. You don't need to do this all the time but enough to support children in what they are doing. When children are moving their bodies for enjoyment, you can describe their movement. "Wow, you're really reaching your arms up high." You are adding to their vocabulary and making them conscious of all the parts of their bodies that they are moving. As children get older, they can still benefit from this when they are trying a new skill. For preschoolers, it might be skipping. For schoolagers, it might be pitching a ball.

You can do this to help children be aware of their social choices too. "You're holding the doll in front of Jamilla. It looks like you want her to play dolls with you." This helps the first child be aware of what they are doing and cues Jamilla that she is being asked (nonverbally) to play. You may have to add some redirection in your announcing. "You want her to play dolls with you. It hurts her if you hit her with the doll. You can hold the doll in front of her, and we can ask." This play-by-play helps the child learn socially acceptable ways to interact with others.

As children get older, most of them get more adept at nonverbal communication, but everyone needs help sometimes (some more than others). Teachers can continue to help with the play-by-play announcing often done for toddlers. The teacher can intersperse direct instruction as well.

A teacher may help a child enter into roughhousing by first playing chase with the child. Chase has universally recognized rules. Children don't need to speak the same language to play chase. Monkeys and canines also play this game. Children build trust when they play chase together, which may allow children to play other games that may involve more physical contact.

While much of roughhousing involves communication with the body, the voice is very much a part of the play as well. Players frequently make interjections such as "ooh" "ahh" or "oh" when they play, which serves to keep the play going. Players often use loud voices (often deeper in pitch) to take on a particular role. Players also may roar like an animal or monster as part of the play. This is especially true for boys. One study found that boys made these "play noises" about three times as often as girls (Smith and Connolly 1972). This play noise is very much a part of the play, but it is often the most disruptive part of the play for non-players. I think it is important to recognize this and try to find a happy medium.

Because big body play relies mostly on nonverbal communication, children can play even if they don't speak the same language. This is especially true for chasing games where the rules are fairly universal. If the play includes rough-housing, the children need to learn to say and understand the word *stop*, whether in English or another language. Children speaking a nondominant language can have a hard time interacting with dominant-language speakers until they learn enough of the language. Big body play allows interaction and thus bonding earlier than many types of play.

Teachers Reading Body Language

Just as children learn to read body language, teachers do as well. Sometimes even we can get it wrong. Teachers who don't allow roughhousing often worry about the play turning into fighting or mistakenly read the play as fighting. As teachers allow roughhousing and chase, they need to read the children more accurately.

Children will exhibit a "play face" (Brannigan and Humphries, 1972), or at the very least, a relaxed, neutral face. At times they may have exaggerated scowls to mimic aggression, but the muscles are relaxed enough to switch to a smile every so often. The tone of voice is higher pitched. Teachers can also watch to see if children are moving toward each other rather than trying to get away. If one child or more is getting mad, the pitch of the voices will go lower, and the face and hands will tense up. If they are standing, they crouch down a bit in a boxer stance.

Roughhousing does not turn into aggression any more than any other type of play. What is more common is a child getting a minor injury. In quality rough-housing, the other children will pause and check in with the injured child. Depending on the child, a teacher may need to help calm the child. Frequently, the child will want to join the play again after calming down. This cycle of stop-ping, checking in, and starting back up actually helps children build a sense of trust and empathy with one another. It also leads to impulse control as children self-handicap as they continue to play. Self-handicapping is when children adjust their physical effort to match the others they are engaging with. A larger child will hold back when roughhousing with a smaller child. The children learn more about one another, and we can learn more about them when we read their body language.

Exploration and Movement

We all have a desire to explore the world around us. This fuels our desire to move. I remember watching my daughter as an infant as she stretched for a toy that was just out of reach. Before she knew it, she had rolled over. Later she started crawling by following our dog around the house. Eventually she took her first steps walking from one grandma to the other, stopping briefly for a hug and kiss before turning around and walking back.

As children move, they discover the world around them. The more they discover, the more they learn, which encourages them to move even more (Gill Connell, pers. comm.). This exploration is the basis of cognitive development. Children observe and make sense of their environment by interacting with it. Soon they are comparing objects, sorting, measuring, and counting them. They recognize patterns in the world around them. Principles of physics, such as momentum, start with movement, usually running into objects or other people. They make predictions and test them out.

They do this regardless of what we are teaching. In fact, many "interruptions" to a classroom are actually children investigating: How far can I lean back on my chair? What happens if I throw this toy? How much toilet paper can fit in the drain? Children have an endless desire to explore. We can try to restrict this as teachers, knowing it is a hopeless pursuit. Or we can give them an environment rich in open-ended materials and let them explore.

It all starts with movement, but movement continues to be an essential part of development. If we want children to learn, we need to let them move. We also need to listen to more than just the words of children. Children express themselves as much through movement as they do through words. When we take the time to watch them, we "hear" them in ways we would otherwise miss.

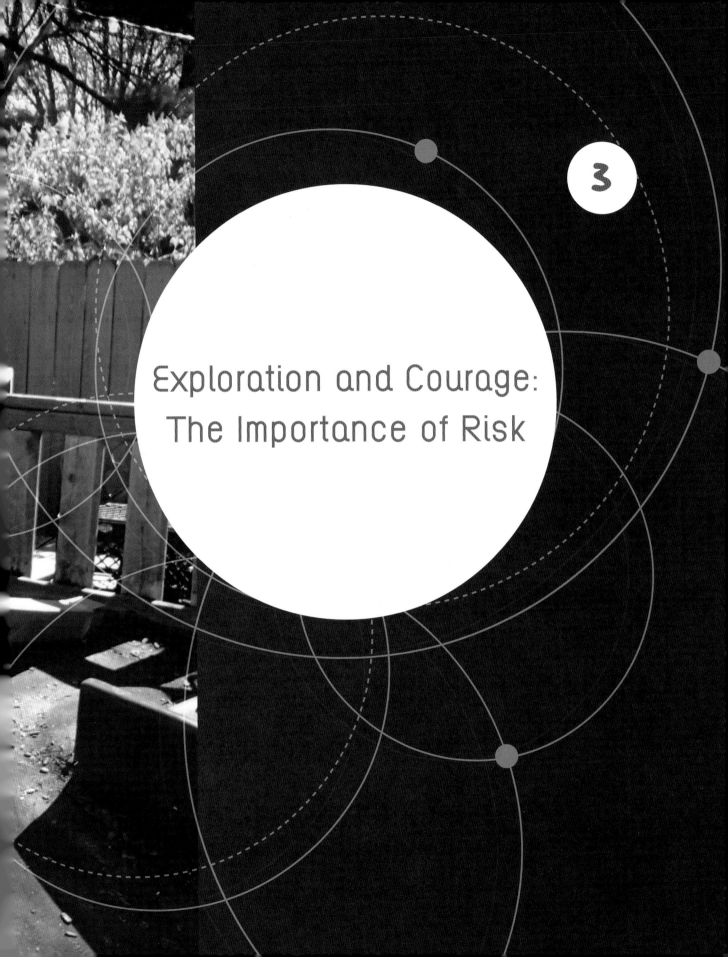

Exploration and Courage:
The Importance of Risk

As children actively explore, they take on more risks. Risk is an inherent part of exploration and discovery. Taking risks, no matter how small, builds courage in children. The word *risk* has a negative connotation in the adult world. The term *courageous play* rather than *risky play* may help adults focus on the positive benefits of play that may involve some risk (Gill Connell, pers. comm.). Being courageous makes play more exciting. For example, balancing on a piece of wood can be fun even if you are only two inches off the ground, but if you put that same board a foot or two in the air, it becomes more thrilling and more enticing for most preschoolers.

Risk is a natural part of life. Being alive means you are at risk of injury or death. Of course this doesn't stop us from going on with our lives. We simply learn to manage risk. Some risks are so remote, we learn that there is no need to think about them. Other risks we learn to minimize with minor adjustments to our behaviors, such as looking before we cross the street. Children also need to learn how to cope with daily risk, gradually gaining courage. Children learn this by engaging in physically challenging and adventurous play (Willoughby 2011).

In other words, big body play or rough-and-tumble play is not only fun and good for children's physical health, it is also good for their emotional development and sense of self. Some of the many benefits of risky play for children include "direct experience of consequence of actions," "awareness of the capabilities and

the limits of their bodies," "emotional resilience," "the ability to assess risk," and "learning to be resourceful, creative and inventive" (Willoughby 2011, 9).

One way to illustrate this is to look at the risk from bodies of water. Children are at risk for drowning when they play in or near water. One strategy to keep children safe would be to keep them away from water. Ultimately, this would be more dangerous because at some point children will find themselves near a body of water and will not have a sense of what they can and cannot do in the water and how to keep themselves safe. A better strategy for managing risk is to teach them to swim. They can learn to be confident in the water. They are less likely to take unnecessary risks because they have developed confidence and courage regarding water safety. The same can be said for other play that involves risk. A child may get a scrape or a bruise or even—on rare occasion—a broken bone, but they will learn from the experience.

Fear of Risk

There seems to be a misunderstanding about risk in the United States, not just in early childhood programs but in our society in general. There is no distinction made between hazards and risks. Joan Almon (2013), author of *Adventure: The Value of Risk in Children's Play*, defines hazards as dangers that a child cannot easily see or predict. A risk is something that a child can see and can perform an assessment thereof. For example, if a child is running on uneven ground, they

will compensate for a slight dip or a rock or a root. If, however, they are running on a commercial playground surface that is completely flat, and there is one spot where the surface has a hole, the child wouldn't expect the uneven surface, and a fall is more likely. Both have risk, but the commercial surface has an unexpected dip, so it could be considered a hazard.

We also have to think about perceived risk versus real risk (or hazard). For example, children under the age of five die from a car accident ten times more often than a fall. Children between the ages of five and nine are more than sixty times as likely to die from a car accident as a fall (Centers for Disease Control and Prevention 2014). Yet I frequently hear adults telling children not to climb, and I have yet to hear a parent warn their child about riding in a car. There is a perception that climbing is more dangerous, but it depends how you define danger. It is true that children may get a scrape or bruise from falling, and it is highly unlikely that they would get a similar injury from riding in a car. However, they are more likely to be seriously injured or die in a car accident than by falling. In other words, the likelihood of being hurt from a fall is greater than a car accident, but the severity of the injury is far less.

More importantly, a child has no control over the safety of riding in a car, but they have quite a bit of agency when it comes to the safety of climbing. The child needs to develop their courage and innate sense of assessing risk.

This innate sense of assessing risk happens quite early. Infants avoid drop-offs as young as six months, as illustrated in the "visual cliff" studies of psychologists Eleanor Gibson and R. D. Walk. Children at all ages tend to approach new physical challenges slowly. For example, when confronted by a new climbing structure, children will climb partway and come down. They will repeat this, going a little farther each time until they get to the top. Not only are children capable of assessing risk, risk is an important part of their development.

Educator Sara Knight puts it this way: "Without opportunities to challenge themselves, children's understanding of safety will not move forward" (Knight

2011, 16). One way to do this is to "make the risk as apparent as possible" (Willoughby 2011, 8). For example, children can see the risk of climbing higher.

Problems arise when children do not get enough experience assessing risk because the adults around them minimize risk for them. If parents always dress their children, the children do not learn how to dress themselves. The same is true for risk assessment. On the other hand, parents and teachers will often "help" children by lifting them up on a climber, tree branch, monkey bars, or other structure. Perhaps it would help some parents or teachers to think of the words *daring* or *courage* instead of *risk*. We can't teach children courage by "helping" them climb a tree. This circumvents children's own understanding of their limits.

Here is how Ellen Beate Hansen Sandseter (2013, 49), a Norwegian researcher, describes the preventive benefits of taking risks: "Child safety policy might want to focus more on the preventative effect of letting children learn how to assess and handle risks themselves as a means of injury *prevention* [emphasis added]." Allowing children to engage in risky play can actually make children safer if used as a learning opportunity. This can happen anywhere: in the classroom, in other parts of a building, in your program's outdoor space, or out in the neighborhood. Playgrounds—whether at your program or a nearby park—probably represent the biggest opportunities for children to learn how to assess risk.

Playgrounds

Playgrounds in the United States have been heavily regulated in the past few decades because of some high-profile injuries and deaths. Children climbing on playground equipment present a risk of falling. Running on the playground also increases the chances of falling. It is true that the most common reason for a child to visit the emergency room is because of falls (at playgrounds and elsewhere), but it is rare for that to happen with teachers present (Centers for Disease Control and Prevention 2014). One study found that, according to the Consumer Product Safety Commission (CPSC), between 1990 and 2000, 10 percent of falls resulting in emergency room visits happened in "commercial daycare settings," and 3 percent of the falls happened in "home daycare settings," (Tinsworth and McDonald 2001, ii). In other words, child care settings account

for a small minority of injuries. In the United Kingdom, more children are injured from playing badminton than from playgrounds (Ball, Gill, and Spiegal 2012). This is not to say that we shouldn't try to minimize injury, but I think our fear of our students getting injured is out of proportion with reality.

Some of the injuries occur due to equipment failure, so we can minimize risk by making sure structures are in good shape (National Program for Playground Safety, accessed 2015). We also have to make sure that kids learn how to use the equipment. The fact that so many of the accidents happen at home, where it is more likely that children are not closely supervised on climbing equipment, tells me that we need to help children learn to self-assess risk on climbing structures so they can make good choices on their own.

While I do not want any child to get injured, I also know that injuries will happen. All I can hope for is that by minimizing the risk and helping children learn to be confident in their ability to assess risk, they will become courageous. This requires them to experience climbing, jumping, and taking some small risks. We need to make sure that our playgrounds encourage these skills. Kids should be able to climb several ways, balance, and even jump from these structures.

I also want to mention our ultimate fear, the death of a child. Deaths on playgrounds are extremely rare. The Consumer Product Safety Commission found that between 2001 and 2008, only forty children died in playground-related incidents. More than half of these deaths resulted from hangings or other asphyxiations (National Program for Playground Safety, accessed 2015). As sad as this is, almost all asphyxiation deaths are preventable by making sure there are no entrapments on playground equipment and that children do not have drawstrings on their hoods or other clothing. Entrapments are considered holes big enough for a child's head to fit through but too small for their shoulders. Entrapments are a hazard because children cannot predict the danger posed by the gap.

Another danger that can be fairly serious is injury to the head and neck. At the same time, children love being upside down. If children are hanging upside down from a height of a few feet, a fall could be devastating. If you have a horizontal ladder (often referred to as monkey bars in the United States), or other bars that are up high, you may want to have children use their hands only (not hang from their legs or feet). You can also offer to spot children if the height seems reasonable. Mats designed for rock climbing offer a little more protection and certainly could be used. Just as important, anytime you prohibit something, you must find a new way to meet the needs of the child. How can children hang upside down safely? Can you have a bar that is low enough to hang upside down? Can they sit on chairs upside down? Also, very few injuries occur on playgrounds that don't involve commercial equipment, so you can give children plenty of ways to play (National Program for Playground Safety, accessed 2015). (For more ideas on what you can do with your playground, see pages 159–63.)

Big Body Play without Equipment

I also hear teachers worry about kids getting hurt when they engage in rough-and-tumble play even if it does not involve playground equipment. But what do they mean by *getting hurt*? After all, we let kids use scissors even though they could get hurt. As stated above, few playground injuries don't involve playground equipment. Of course this information only counts injuries resulting in emergency room visits. Teachers and other adults often worry about scrapes, bruises, and scratches. It is true that these minor injuries will occur and probably more often when children engage in rough-and-tumble play. These injuries are minor, and children gain so much from them in terms of physical, social, and emotional development.

Finally, I have found that some teachers will point out that this play leads to someone crying. Admittedly, I have found that kids cry when playing rough. I have also found that just as often, kids will cry while playing most anything: pretend play (family, superheroes, zoo, boat, beauty shop, and so on), drawing, looking at books, going up or down stairs, block building. In fact, I cannot think of a type of play that doesn't result in crying when more than one young child is involved. As

long as teachers value the play (and the children's experiences), we can allow various types of play, including big body play, and address children's needs.

Children cry for a variety of reasons. Sometimes children cry because they are frustrated when they are unable to achieve a self-imposed goal, such as building a tall block structure. A teacher can help them work through this and reassess their process. Other times they cry because they are sad or mad, and they need a teacher to help them work through these strong emotions.

Other times they cry because they get hurt. But even when a child cries because they are hurt, there are a few distinct cries. Some children will cry to indicate that they are experiencing some discomfort and want the play to stop. For example, when children roughhouse, one child might cry, and the others might stop roughhousing. The child may pause for a few breaths and then start roughhousing again. This child wasn't injured. They simply needed a break, and they weren't able to verbalize their need. Eventually children usually learn to say, "Stop." In essence this cry is a test to see if the playmates are trustworthy (see pages 74–76 for a discussion on trust). Occasionally children may cry because they are truly injured and need a teacher's assistance. I find this happens about as often from roughhousing as it does from going on a neighborhood walk or playing with blocks.

Confidence

Children like to take risks, some more than others. Adults can make sure the risk is acceptable, but we can't eliminate all risk, nor should we try. Children gain a lot from risk, including confidence. Too often we try to boost children's confidence by heaping praise on them. But saying "Good job!" a hundred times is fairly meaningless compared to letting a child climb a tree or run up a slide. The challenge followed by the accomplishment (maybe after several tries) is much more fulfilling. When children set a self-imposed goal and then accomplish it, they are encouraged to set more goals for themselves and further their development. Children who try something only because an adult will heap praise on them are often reluctant to try new things on their own.

It is true that children may get a few more bumps and bruises, but they will make up for that in pride. But that's not all . . .

A few years ago I had taken my preschool class to a picnic at an assisted living facility that we visit every other week. I was on one end of the outdoor area playing parachute games with several children. On the other side, some of the children were going up and down a rocky slope (maybe four feet high) that led to a dry overflow ditch. One of the workers from the facility asked if that was okay. My teacher-brain immediately thought I shouldn't let them, but I thought about what I had been learning about the need for risk, so I said, "Maybe I should go over and see."

I walked over and watched the kids go up and down on the rocks. As their confidence grew, some of the kids quickened their pace. I did mention that some rocks might be loose, but I doubt anyone heard me. They continued going up and down for about five minutes before sitting down for food.

I know that if this happened five years earlier, I would have stopped it and maybe had them go down on the grassy part of the slope. But they chose the rocks because it was a challenge and riskier and therefore more fun. They ran for about five minutes, smiling the whole time. Not only did it boost their confidence in themselves, but it boosted my confidence in them as well.

Assessing Risk to Promote Courage

If you decide to allow for riskier play, how do you make sure you are still doing everything you can to keep kids safe? The first step is to move closer before you tell them to stop. Ask yourself if what you are witnessing is a risk, which is something children can easily understand and adjust their behaviors to accordingly, or if it is a hazard, something that is not so obvious. If it is a hazard, then you can stop the play and explain why. For example, roughhousing while eating food is a choking hazard, which children might not realize. If it is a risk, quickly decide what the risks and benefits are. If the risk far outweighs the benefits, you can stop the play and talk to the children about your concerns. If it is truly a risk and not a hazard, the children can often find ways to minimize the risk. For example, if kids start roughhousing in the bathroom, you could point out all the hard surfaces. Ask them if they can think of a place that has softer surfaces in case they fall down.

It is important not to think of the risks in isolation, but rather in conjunction with the benefits. Remember that many reasonable risks give kids a sense of confidence, help them avoid taking unreasonable risks, and can keep them safer in the long run. There are also cognitive, creative, physical, and social benefits to many activities that may be risky.

If you have decided that the benefits outweigh the risks, watch the children to see if they seem to be self-assessing the risk and making adjustments to their play. Are they moving away from other children who aren't playing? Are they varying the intensity, pulling back just as the play verges on being out of control? I think you will find that once you look for this behavior, you will see children assessing risk and accounting for it quite frequently.

If children are getting a little too excited to stay in control (such as bumping into a table or another person who is not playing), you can remind them of the guidelines of taking care of one another and ask how they can make sure they are in control so as not to accidentally interfere with the play of others. When you talk with them, be sure to ask them to look to see if there is anything they need to be aware of. You should also point to where you want them to look. Boys tend to need to use their visual sense to more accurately assess risk. You may also need to have them look at the guidelines posted in your room.

If a child is taking on a physical challenge that has some risk, approach it the same way as described above. See if they are self-assessing the risk. If they seem

I visited Dodge Nature Preschool in Saint Paul, Minnesota, and saw children balancing on a slackline (with a second rope to hold on to). I saw children climb a steep hill, some using a rope and some merely stepping carefully. Some even ran down the hill at the end. There was a giant log that a few children straddled and slowly made their way across, while others crawled and a few walked across, arms out to keep their balance. There were smiles and laughter. These kids had so much confidence.

This confidence is nurtured by the teachers, Kristenza Nelson and David Longsdorf, who are constantly assessing the risks and benefits of situations the children encounter. They help children build on their skills while helping them reflect on their abilities.

For example, the slackline was about one foot off the ground. At the beginning of the year, the teachers let one child on at a time, and a teacher stayed close and verbally encouraged the child. As the children became more comfortable, the teachers allowed the children to go

continued on next page

on together. Some children chose to wait until they were the only ones on, but most found it both physically challenging and a great way to bond with friends.

Kristenza and David showed as much care and concern for these children as any teachers I have seen. But they also showed trust in the children. And the children rose to the challenge. The teachers know that a child may fall and scrape a knee or elbow. They have bandages if that happens. But the benefits far outweigh this risk. The children develop a sense of balance, build closer friendships, persist in a task that seems difficult at first, and gain self-confidence. Oh, and they have fun too.

to be stuck, you can start by letting them know you are watching. This might give them enough confidence to take a risk and finish their task.

If they seem to be moving too quickly without enough deliberation, you can let them know you notice them. Start with something like, "Look how high you are!" Then you can ask if they are aware of the risks in as neutral a way as possible, such as, "Have you ever climbed this high before?" Once you have begun the conversation, you can voice your concerns if you still have them. "I notice you are moving quickly; I'm worried you might slip. Is there anything you can do to make sure you don't slip?" Let them problem solve as much as possible.

If they do get stuck and ask for help getting down, verbally reassure them that you are right there. Then you can help talk them through how they get down. Unless it's an emergency, don't help them physically. They may be scared, but if they physically do it themselves, they will have a better idea how to do it next time.

Never lift children into places they are unable to get to themselves. They cannot assess how to deal with the height if they haven't climbed it. You can help talk them through climbing themselves, or you can find them something else to climb on where they may have more success, but you want them to develop an internal sense of how to navigate these types of risks.

Steps to Assess Risk

Play with potential risk

⬇

1. Approach and assess

If it's relatively safe, continue to monitor.

If serious injury is possible, move to step 2.

⬇

2. Risk-benefit analysis

If benefits outweigh risk, continue to monitor.

If not, move to step 3.

⬇

3. Risk discussion with children

Make any changes to minimize risk and monitor.

If risk can't be minimized, move to step 4.

⬇

4. Alternative activities

Any other activities that can meet the same needs?

Any other places where activity might be possible?

Risk-Benefit Analysis

As you start to look for the benefits of risky play, you can be proactive in assessing any possible risks in your program. Again, you are not only analyzing the risk, but also the benefits. This risk-benefit analysis does not need to be complicated. This is how risk analysis is categorized in *Managing Risk in Play Provision*, published by the National Children's Bureau in England:

Striking the right balance between protecting children from the most serious risks and allowing them to reap the benefits of play is not about eliminating risk. Nor is it about complicated methods of calculating risks or benefits. In essence, play is a safe and beneficial activity. Sensible adult judgments are all that is generally required to derive the best benefits to children whilst ensuring that they are not exposed to unnecessary risk. (Ball, Gill, and Spiegal 2012)

You can include any activity that could pose a risk, including playing with blocks, going on field trips, and so on. Identify what the specific risk is, that is, the potential injury. Then you identify the benefits. Once you have done this, you can decide on strategies that would minimize the risk. This may be as simple as reminding the children of the risk. It could also involve specific procedures for teachers or altering equipment. The purpose of the document is to find a way to allow the activities unless there really is no way to make them reasonably safe.

Sample Risk-Benefit Assessment Table

Activity	Benefit	Risk	Level of risk (high/medium/low)	Action to minimize risk	Revised level of risk
Playing with sticks	Creativity, problem solving, cooperative play	Poking or scraping another child	Medium	Brainstorm with children how to use sticks safely	Low

This is one example of how you might assess risks and benefits. It is similar to the way you would assess risk during play, but the written documentation allows you to reflect more intentionally, as well as to record how you have minimized risk. The risk-benefit analysis should be done for any activity that is likely to occur on a daily basis. If you are in a program with more than one teacher, the risk-benefit analysis is a great way to make sure you are on the same page. If you are not yet comfortable with risky play, you can breathe a sigh of relief knowing you have already considered the dangers and identified ways to minimize the risk.

Risk-benefit analyses can look different but essentially have the same basic elements. Some may use a numbered rating system or identify who will actually take the action to reduce risk. In the example table, I listed the particular activity. Then I listed the benefits and risks. After that, I could gauge the level of risk. Finally, I identified ways to minimize the risk. Often, simply having children talk about the risks beforehand is all that is needed. Sometimes you and the children may have to brainstorm ways to make the activity safer. Either way, including children in this process not only makes this activity safer, but it also models for them how to assess risk.

Situations will arise that are not listed in your risk-benefit analysis. When that happens, you can rely on the process on page 68, steps to allow risk.

Policy on Risk

As you allow children to play more freely, you will want to make sure you have a policy that states that you consider risk an essential part of play. You may also need to add a statement about risk in any parent handbook. We currently live in an overprotective environment, and many parents will assume that you avoid any activity that has the slightest risk unless you clearly state otherwise. You want to be sure to emphasize that risk is part of healthy development.

Children want to be courageous, so they are attracted to risk. Nothing beats the joy of successfully taking a risk. While we can minimize risks, we cannot eliminate them. Risk is a part of being alive, and children need to have the courage to deal with risk. Our job isn't to keep them from falling. It's to help them up and hug them when they do fall. The real risk is that children won't explore or challenge themselves. If they know how to self-assess and minimize risk, they can be lifelong explorers, confident in their own abilities.

Sample Policy

This center respects children's innate interest in risk. We allow children to take reasonable risk based on each child's development as a means of injury prevention and opportunity for learning.

4

Courage and Trust:
Rough-and-Tumble Play
and Roughhousing

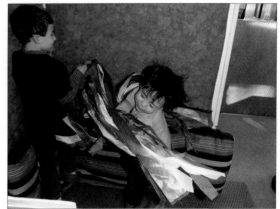

One of the more difficult things for many teachers of young children to deal with is rough-and-tumble play. It feels chaotic and loud. When I first started teaching, I tried to keep rough-and-tumble play out of the classroom. I would tell children to wait until we went outside. This proved to be ineffective. The kids were showing me what physical needs they had right now. Rough-and-tumble play (and other big body play) actually helps children regulate so they can participate in group activities in the classroom (Carlson 2011a). It provides resistance to their muscles, which has a calming effect for many children. It also makes their brains more active and alert.

Ultimately, I found my room was less chaotic and the kids were more in control of their actions when I allowed some big body play in the classroom. Rough-and-tumble play requires a balance of trust and courage. When kids engage in this type of play, they learn how to deal with risk and how to trust others.

Courage and Trust

While all rough-and-tumble play involves some trust, chase and roughhousing require more because they involve some contact with other children. Of course, with young children, any activity can lead to contact with other children. It is sometimes hard to distinguish dancing or spinning from roughhousing. For the sake of simplicity, I will use the term *roughhousing* to include any play that involves physical contact, even if it is incidental. Children need to have a sense of trust and courage to comfortably play in this way or else it can result in anger and conflict.

The more contact involved, the more trust involved. Children who don't know one another usually play chase rather than tackling. The act of roughhous-

ing can build trust between participants. Children put themselves in a vulnerable position, and the other players follow the rules. If children are playing chase and they haven't agreed to tackle one another, then each child expects to be tagged with an open hand. If the rules are followed, all the children are showing impulse control. The same children may engage in play with more physical contact if they play again or if the game continues for a significant amount of time.

Children who know one another well may use roughhousing to maintain social cohesion and trust among themselves. It is important to note that this play fighting (or roughhousing) may sometimes result in children crying or getting minor injuries, such as scrapes or bruises. The success of roughhousing is not based on the presence or absence of injury or tears but rather on the response of those involved. If someone does get hurt, are the other players empathetic? Do they stop and check in with the injured? Do they try to cheer them up or help them up? Or do they taunt them or ignore them? In essence, do they show they are trustworthy?

Some children will use words such as "Are you okay?" or "Sorry" or they will try to make jokes to make the person laugh. Other children will use nurturing physical contact, such as a hand on the shoulder, a hug, or handing them a stuffed animal or other comfort object.

Sometimes the child who caused the injury will feel guilty and will try hiding or get defensive ("I didn't mean to!"). These children are not necessarily trying to ignore the injured child but simply have their own feelings that need to be addressed. Teachers can help these children by acknowledging those feelings. Then help guide them to actions they can take to help the other child. The first few times, the child will probably need the teacher to simply model the behavior (verbally check in, offer physical comfort). Eventually the teacher can remind the child verbally and have them do the check-in.

"You seem sad (upset) that you hurt ____. Sometimes we hurt others without meaning to. When that happens, we can see if there's anything we can do to help. I'll show you." You do not need to force children to say they are sorry. Saying "Sorry" is different than apologizing. An apology requires children to understand that their actions affect others and that intentions and results can be very different. The apology needs to come from the child. If children are forced to say they are sorry, they may feel victimized or misunderstood by the teacher. Both children should feel good about the aftercare that happens when someone is injured. This will build trust among children and between the children and teacher.

It is also important to point out that children under the age of six often have a hard time distinguishing between actions that are accidental and intentional. If they are hurt, they assume there was intention. Conversely, a child who accidentally hurts someone will have a hard time understanding they are responsible since it wasn't their intention. Toddlers will probably not even understand that they were the cause of the injury since they have little understanding of cause and effect. There is often a great disconnect between each child's perception. Conflict resolution with the teacher acting as mediator allows children to hear both sides of the story. Gradually children can gain an understanding that just because they got hurt doesn't mean someone tried to hurt them. At the same time, just because they didn't intentionally hurt someone, it doesn't mean they weren't responsible for the injury and don't need to help the other child.

While children learn to trust one another through physical play, they can also build trust with other physical contact, such as hugs, hand-holding, and the like. As children get older, they may play sports that involve body contact with children they don't know because there are defined rules. Trust is also built through playing, singing, and talking together, but physical contact often plays a part. As mentioned earlier (pages 40–43), touch is essential for social-emotional growth.

Other Types of Big Body Play

Now I want to look at other types of physical play. I use the term *big body play* here to include more types of play than the phrase *rough-and-tumble play* (see pages 11–14). All of them involve some amount of courage. As we have seen, roughhousing requires a fair amount of trust in others. Other activities, such as playing catch, can involve trust in smaller ways. Other play requires taking risk with one's own physical capabilities (e.g., running without falling). All of the play is vigorous, but some also involves contact with other children or objects.

When I started teaching, I found it easier to get kids involved in noncontact vigorous play, such as dancing, chasing, and climbing. I knew children needed to move their bodies, and I thought I was meeting that need.

I now realize that children need contact. That contact can be gentle, such as hugs and cuddling. It can also be more vigorous, such as roughhousing. Either way, it offers resistance like the "heavy work" discussed in chapter 2 (Naomi Siegal, pers. comm.). How much of that contact is gentle and how much is rough depends on the child, but all children need some of both. I find it helps a lot of teachers to think about the touch involved in a hug—the chest, arms, and tummy—and then think of how roughhousing can provide that same touch.

I often see children who seem to act impulsively, pushing other children for no obvious reason, touching everything in reach. Many of these children are not prone to cuddling with others. I find roughhousing with these children helps them self-regulate and act less impulsively.

Kevin and Matt, both three-year-olds, are in the loft. They are pretending to fight monsters. Brenna enters the loft. Kevin says, "A monster!" Kevin and Matt start pushing and kicking Brenna. A teacher comes over and gets in between the children. She guides the children through conflict resolution. The teacher helps them find a way to play without hurting each other but is understandably worried about the way Kevin and Matt treated Brenna so violently.

The teacher had been adding more physical play throughout the day, such as jumping up and down before sitting down for large-group time and dancing to music before lunchtime. It seemed to help a bit, but obviously Kevin and Matt needed more. The next day, I came in to play with Kevin and Matt. They were back in the loft where Jenny and Hank were kings (a "boy king" and a "girl king"). Kevin and Matt were climbing over each other, starting to play physically. A few more kids came in to play, and I was wondering if Kevin and Matt would start pushing or hitting. Then Hank told me I was the knight. I asked if I should battle the dragon. He said I should. I told Kevin and Matt I was scared of dragons and wondered if they would help. Kevin stood tall and said, "I'm not scared of dragons!"

We went out of the loft. I pretended a shelf was the dragon. We each approached the dragon and swung our fists. Then I picked up a big pillow and said, "Here comes another dragon." I pushed it into Kevin. He started pushing back and growling. Then Matt joined in. I pushed just enough to keep them from pushing me over. They kept pushing, so I roared and shook the pillow as I pushed. We pushed back-and-forth for about five minutes. Sometimes I would fall back and say, "You defeated the dragon." But then I would push them again. As they pushed, I would sometimes reach around the pillow and grab them, essentially hugging them with a pillow in between us. They continued to push vigorously.

After about ten minutes, it was cleanup time. They cleaned up and the teacher reported the day went better for them (compared to the day before). I decided I needed to come in once a week to model this more full-contact play for the teachers. The fact that these two kids met my force with equal force for such a long time made me think they weren't getting enough of this type of contact.

Types of Big Body Play

Contact with other children

- rolling on the ground with body contact
- pulling other player
- grabbing another person
- banging body into another body
- wrestling (lifting another's body, rolling on another person)
- pile on (leaning, sitting, etc.)
- pushing another child
- open-hand slap
- tickling
- holding hands

Noncontact motions with or without other children

- running
- chasing
- hitting motions
- kicking motions
- twirling
- falling
- rolling around on ground without contact
- hitting self

Motions with objects (and possibly other people)

- jumping on an object
- kicking an object
- making crashing motions with a held object
- throwing an object
- banging one's body into a fixed object (e.g., a wall)
- making hitting motions while holding an object
- pretending to shoot while holding an object (or pointing hand)
- crashing body into an object
- hitting others with a soft object, such as a foam tube (Carlson 2011a)

Chase and Other Noncontact Big Body Play

Chase is one of the most universal games in existence. The rules are pretty basic and are understood across cultures and many species, as illustrated in my story about the toddlers and the wolf in chapter 1. In fact, this is usually one of the first games that children who don't know one another will play. As they play, they learn whether the other children are trustworthy with little risk involved.

The basic game involves a chaser and someone to be chased. Often people play with one chaser and several being chased. Sometimes there are several chasers. If a game of chase is happening, other children can join in by simply running away from the chaser. As children get older, they often put a theme around the game. Variations of chase include hide-and-seek, predator and prey, shark attack, ghost in the graveyard, manhunt, and many more. It is interesting to note how many of the themes given to chase involve hunting (and being hunted). Many believe that this type of play originated as a way to learn how to avoid being hunted and to learn hunting skills.

While this game may have an evolutionary origin, most of us do not have to worry about being hunted, and those of us who hunt use guns where tracking, hiding, and good aim are more important than our ability to chase down prey. What does happen when we play chase is that we get a burst of energy. Our hearts race both from running and the feeling of pursuit. This burst of energy also "provides an unparalleled stimulus, creating an environment in which the brain is ready, willing, and able to learn" (Ratey 2008, 10).

Perhaps most importantly, people who play games of chase gain a sense of trust, and over time they can bond. Our bodies respond to the game as if we are being hunted, but the chaser usually simply tags the other person (unless there is a mutual agreement to have more body contact). If the people being chased are faster than the chaser, they will often slow down until the chaser is close. This makes the game more exciting for all. When a person is tagged, it is expected that they will follow the agreed upon rule. If there are no agreed upon rules, usually the person tagged becomes the chaser. As children follow these rules, they show themselves to be trustworthy. Often at the end of chase, the players talk among themselves as they rest their bodies (even if they didn't know one another at the beginning of the game).

How to Teach Young Children to Play Chase

Very young children (usually two- and three-year-olds) may need some direct instruction to learn the rules of chase. This is also true of children who are still learning to trust others. The first thing to learn is that if you see children playing chase, and you do not want to play, just keep doing what you are doing. Toddlers and young preschoolers will often start running away to avoid the game. This signals to the chaser that they are playing. You can teach them to just stand by and watch the others run past them. You can also teach them to say, "I'm not playing." The fight-flight-or-freeze response is trying to kick in, and you are helping them control that impulse. Once they have a few positive experiences with this, they will probably be able to do it on their own. Children with a history of negative touch will need more success before they are able to control their impulses. They may be worried that they are being attacked and may be more likely to hit the other children in an effort to protect themselves. It helps if you can remind these children how to avoid the game before the kids playing chase get close.

Now that you have taught children how to avoid playing, you can teach them how to join in. Even older preschoolers and young schoolagers will sometimes make the mistake of trying to join a game of chase by stopping the runners and asking if they can join. This actually decreases the likelihood of joining. As mentioned in chapter 3, nonverbal communication is usually more successful. You can teach them to figure out who the chaser is and run away from them. You can also teach them to say, "You can't catch me." If school-age children are involved, there may be a theme to the game, so you may need to tell the child to observe first to find out what you do if you get caught. Depending on the child's ability to pick up on nonverbal communication, you may need to verbalize what you see.

The last thing you may have to teach is how to catch someone appropriately.

Most games require a simple tag, touching with one hand. Very young children are often dealing with controlling how much force to use in different situations. When children are running full speed, it takes a lot of control to tag only gently. They have to match their speed before touching other children. In a mixed-age setting, it often works out that the smaller child might use too much force, but the bigger children can handle it. If a child is bigger but inexperienced with positive touch, they may need more guidance in this area. As always, it helps to verbalize brief instructions before the situation occurs. If the chase game involves tackling, then refer to the instructions for roughhousing to help children use appropriate force.

Big Body Play with Objects

Some big body play involves using objects. These objects may be used solo, such as jumping rope, or used to interact with other children. The objects may be anchored, such as a climbing structure or tree, or they may move.

Children naturally climb and will usually start to climb before they can walk. Infants will start to climb but have little sense of how to gauge how high they can climb and still get down. It is best to have only low objects infants can climb. All children need to climb, and equipment should be offered. The equipment should be anchored so it does not move as a child climbs. The height of the equipment can get higher as children gain skills and ability.

Children also use objects to push, pull, spin, swing, wave, and so on. This could include pushing vehicles, such as wagons or push toys. Children often pull on just about any object that two children can get a grip on. As long as both children are having fun, this can be a great way for children to interact and test their strength in a less physical way than roughhousing. Sometimes a child will pull on another child's hat or other possession. This can be done as a way to test trust. The child may initiate it to show they are playing a game but will give back the article

when they are done. Of course sometimes the other child will not like this game. Using the guideline "We take care of each other," the child should be able to ask for the item back or have a teacher back them up. If both children seem to be enjoying this tug-of-war as a game, you can let them play so they can develop that sense of trust. If you are unsure of the child's feelings, you can ask and remind both of them of the guideline.

Children may also use objects to strike one another. This type of play is similar to roughhousing but involves some type of object. Usually it is something

long and thin and is used like a sword. Rolled up paper, cardboard tubes, and pool noodles are often used. These objects can be swung, and much like pillows, they rarely hurt. I find that children who don't roughhouse are especially attracted to pool noodles. It gives them a chance to really swing their arms and get that same physical bonding that happens with roughhousing with little risk of injury. Children will use sticks and other hard objects, but I feel the risk of injury is too great, especially when pool noodles work so well.

Children will also strike one another with pillows and balls. I often find that pillow fights are a great way for teachers who may be reluctant to roughhouse to get involved in rough play. You can buy pillows for patio furniture at the end of summer at many home and garden supply stores fairly inexpensively. These pillows can be surface cleaned fairly easily. You can also buy or make simple pillows. They will need to be washed regularly and may get a bit misshapen, but they still work well for pillow fights.

Ball Play

Balls are another favorite to throw. School-age children often play dodgeball, the object of which is to throw the ball so that it hits another child. I find that younger children are more likely to have a pretend scenario that incorporates throwing balls at one another. Other objects that can be thrown at other children include crumpled-up paper, cloth balls, rolled up socks, and bath poufs.

Of course balls get used in other ways as well. Balls are thrown, caught, kicked, or hit with hands or with an object, such as a paddle, racket, or bat. It's important to think about how these different skills are developed to effectively support children in this play. For older schoolagers, you can simply think of sports that incorporate the skill in question. For example, throwing works best with a ball the size of a baseball. Catching works well with a ball the size of a basketball, rugby ball, or something similar. Striking a ball requires a small hard ball, perhaps as small as a golf ball or as big as a softball. If we look at why these balls work for each skill, it will be easier to figure out what works for younger children as well.

Children start to drop objects while they are still infants. Some of this motion is probably involuntary, a matter of experimenting with moving their bodies. Many infants soon learn it is a great way to communicate with adult caregivers. "Every time I throw this cup, Mommy comes over and gives it back to me." This social interaction is evident in games of catch later in life. When I was eight and nine, I think I talked to my father more during games of catch than any other time, and in my teen years, I talked to my friends at length while throwing a Frisbee back and forth.

When children become toddlers, many will start trying to throw or roll objects to another person to play a game of catch, rather than simply throwing the object and letting the adult retrieve it. While rolling a ball uses many different motor skills other than throwing, it helps children learn the rules of catch. You aim the ball at the person so they can catch it. They may have to move a little bit but not so much that the ball goes past them. The next rule is that the person catching the ball rolls or throws it back. They don't keep it. Once these rules have been understood, the child can focus on the motor coordination and control required for accuracy.

The trick with toddlers and preschoolers is that the ball that is easiest to learn to throw is not the same as the ball that is easiest to catch. It is easiest to throw a ball that fits in the palm of the hand, and children learn to catch a larger ball with two hands (Gagen, Getchell, and Payne, 2009). This does not mean you can't play catch with a child this age, but it involves the child throwing and you catching. When you throw it back, you want the ball to land near them. The child will watch it, and when it stops they will pick it up.

At this age, even a baseball is usually too big to throw. A tennis ball will work, especially because the surface offers enough friction even if the fingers don't reach around. Cloth balls or rolled up socks also work well. Paper can be scrunched up for the correct size but has so much wind resistance that children

can't get a sense of control. You have to throw the paper hard just to get it to go a relatively short distance. It is also hard to aim since it slows down so quickly, allowing gravity to take over. Older preschoolers may find these challenges fun as they compensate for the differences between the paper and various types of balls.

At first children will throw by simply moving their arm, keeping their legs and trunk stationary. Eventually children will step forward and extend their trunk as they throw, and finally step with the leg opposite their throwing arm and rotate their trunk (Gagen, Getchell, and Payne, 2009). When these changes take place depends on how much experience the individual child has throwing. When I was growing up, the derogatory phrase "throwing like a girl" referred to throwing without leg movement. Any child who has little experience will throw this way. At the time, most girls were not encouraged to throw balls so they did not develop these more advanced skills. Many boys also did not develop these skills, and thus the insult.

Once children have learned the basics of using their whole body for throwing, they can start to throw larger balls, such as basketballs, footballs, or rugby balls. These balls require throwing with one hand, but the other hand is used to balance the ball until the actual throw. Children may try throwing these balls earlier, especially if they have older role models using these balls, but they will use two hands and motions that have little to do with the throwing motion described above.

Catching a ball is more difficult than throwing a ball. After all, you can successfully throw a ball and have it land just about anywhere, but to successfully catch a ball, you have to have your body positioned correctly and move your arms after the ball gets close but before it bounces away. It is easiest to use a ball that is about seven to nine inches and soft (Gagen, Getchell, and Payne 2009). Beanbags work well since they conform to a child's hand, and they travel in a uniform trajectory. Stuffed animals also work well for similar reasons. These are great things to use when a child is learning to catch because they often close their eyes and even turn their head when an object is thrown at them. A soft object will allow them to resist that impulse and visually track the object without fear of getting hit.

Once a child has had some experience visually tracking an object thrown at them, you can use a playground ball, but it should still be about eight inches. It is common to see eighteen- or twenty-two-inch balls on playgrounds, but they are too big for toddlers and preschoolers. If you introduce playground balls for catching, I have found it helpful to bounce the ball to the child. It is less intimidating to have a ball come up to you than it is to have it coming down at you. It also slows down the trajectory a bit but still in a predictable way.

As children are able to track the ball, they can learn to absorb the impact of the ball. They can move their arms in the direction the ball was traveling or turn their body some to slow it down. Children also need to learn to move their body so it is positioned in front of where the ball is headed. Finally, children learn to adjust their hands so they have their fingers pointing up to catch a ball above their waist and pointing down for a ball traveling below their waist. In general, children will learn to catch later than they learn to throw. Even twelve-year-olds will have trouble adjusting their hands correctly (Gagen, Getchell, and Payne 2009).

Older school-age children will have enough dexterity to be able to throw and catch the same ball, but you can still use these tips for younger children to help a child who needs more practice with some of these skills. Once children have some of the basic skills, you can vary the size of the ball or object a bit so they can learn how to accommodate those differences.

The third skill with balls is striking. Striking can include kicking, hitting with a hand, or using another object, such as a mallet, racket, paddle, or bat. No

matter the method used to strike a ball, it is easier to strike a stationary ball than a moving ball.

When learning to kick a ball, it is easiest when the ball is stationary. The easiest ball to kick is between six and nine inches (Gagen, Getchell, and Payne 2009). A gallon milk jug also works well. Children will start by moving one leg only. As they develop their kicking skills, they will also step with the opposite leg first, wind up with their kicking leg, and rotate their torso. These skills will develop only with experience, so children need opportunities to kick. I find that preschoolers may kick balls for a short time, but then they stop chasing after the ball. Usually they can't kick with enough accuracy to kick back and forth with others. This is especially true when the children are not in mixed groups with older children who do have these skills or where soccer is not an important part of their culture.

Preschoolers and younger schoolagers may try kicking a ball at a target, but it will have to be fairly big. You may see if they can hit a fence or wall, for example. You can make a smaller target as they get more accurate. When children are about eight years old or older, they may have enough skill and interest to play a short soccer game.

For preschoolers and younger schoolagers, I find the game Kick the Can encourages children to kick for a sustained period of time. I would use gallon milk jugs for younger children. I have used twelve-ounce cans for older preschoolers as well. The milk jugs don't roll quite as far, so you don't have to run after them as much. I often have the kids kick the can on our neighborhood walks, where we are heading in one direction. While on a sidewalk, there is an obvious (but not too small) target of moving forward. On either side keeps most cans from straying too far. The children also like the sound of the cans or jugs on the sidewalk. I have had children kick cans for about twenty minutes. I have rarely had kids kick balls on the playground for that long.

Soccer balls also work well because they are easier to control than playground balls. Even size 3 soccer balls can be a bit too big for toddlers and young preschoolers. Broomballs work well for these children. They are similar to soccer balls but are about six inches in diameter.

Striking a ball with a hand is difficult for most preschoolers and toddlers. A tetherball, a ball attached to a rope, is easier because it can be hit when it is stationary. Dribbling a basketball is more advanced, but because the trajectory is predictable, it is easier than a game such as volleyball, which requires a person to move their whole body and make controlled contact with the ball. Preschoolers tend to dribble right in front of themselves without leaning their bodies. This often results in the ball bouncing off their toes.

Balloons or beach balls are a good first ball for striking because they move slowly (also making them poor choices for learning to catch where a child needs a uniform trajectory). Children can also strike a ball that is placed on a tee or hung from a rope (like a tetherball) but fastened with Velcro so the ball can still project. As a child is able to strike a ball with their hand, they can start to use paddles. The closer the striking surface is to the hand, the easier it is to hit the ball. Ping-Pong paddles or a similar toy are good first paddles. As children get older, longer paddles can be used. Plastic bats can also be used, but again, shorter bats work better.

Croquet works very well for preschoolers and young schoolagers. The balls are stationary and fairly big. I have found that most preschoolers can't aim the ball they are hitting to play the actual game of croquet, but they can certainly make the balls roll far. You could simply have the kids make the balls go forward as in Kick the Can, or you could ask them to hit the ball past a line that extends the width of the playground. Golf can work the same way, but I find the balls are too small and the clubs need quite a bit of supervision in group care. It could work with a smaller adult-child ratio, such as with a parent and child. Some older preschoolers will be able to hit a moving ball. It helps to have a teacher or older child who can throw the ball gently but in a predictable trajectory.

For any of these skills with balls, children need to be successful more than half the time to keep trying. You will have to gauge the best way for each child to develop these skills. You will also be continuously adjusting as children develop skills. The important thing is to give children these experiences with lots of repetition. It is not enough simply to have balls on the playground.

Young children should be learning these skills independent of a specific sport. Sports such as soccer and tee ball are offered at younger and younger ages. I worry that this could focus too much on a narrow number of skills. My other worry is that the kids with more-developed skills will play more because they can keep the ball longer, leaving the kids with less-developed skills to get less experience. I don't see a need for kids to join a sport before the age of eight. What I think would be more helpful is a session of "freeplay on a field." Instead

One year I had a class of particularly active children. On top of that, I had a four-year-old who could throw a football across the playground right into my hands, bat a pitched ball, and dribble a soccer ball. I have my class engage in investigations where we spend a few weeks studying something in depth. I knew our investigation this year needed to involve movement. I made videos of them playing with balls. I showed them videos and started asking questions about the different types of balls. They had a vague notion that you didn't kick certain balls or throw other ones.

The next day, I set out tennis balls and had the children kick them around. Then I had them throw playground balls. I asked how it went. Then we tried throwing tennis balls and kicking playground balls. Later that day, we watched the video. We spent the next several weeks exploring balls. What was it about the size, bounciness, and smoothness that made each ball ideal for its job? We took apart several balls and tried floating them to find out more about them. We came up with more questions. "Why do golf balls sink and bowling balls float?" "Why are softballs so hard?"

Ultimately, it came down to "How does the ball fit the movements of our bodies?" The kids discovered the basic principles I mentioned in this section. You need to be able to hold a ball you are throwing. It's easier to catch a big ball. A heavy ball rolls straighter than a light, bouncy one.

of coaches, there would be play workers who help children with the skills they are interested in. One area could be kids kicking balls at a soccer net (a big area when there is no goalie or keeper), another area might be kids running around cones, and another area would be kids throwing balls at another soccer net.

Balls and Skills (Gagen, Getchell, and Payne 2009)

Skill	Ideal ball size for learning	Alternatives to balls
Throwing	Fits in palm	Beanbags, stuffed animals, crumpled paper
Catching	7–9"	Large stuffed animal
Kicking	6–9"	Milk jugs, cans
Striking	Light-weight ball	Stick on a tree, crumpled paper

Big Body Play with Contact: Roughhousing, Play Fighting, Wrestling, and Horseplay

Roughhousing, play fighting, wrestling, and horseplay refer to rough play with body contact. While there is no specific definition, I tend to use the term *roughhousing* in my own classroom to refer to rough play that we engage in on a mat or in an area outside away from other types of play (so we don't interfere). I find the terms *wrestling* and *play fighting* don't accurately describe what preschoolers do when they play rough. There are plenty of times where the kids will pile on top of one another and giggle. Or they will hop around near one another. I find the term *horseplay* can be misleading since there are times when kids pretend to be animals, including horses.

Roughhousing for preschoolers often involves pushing, tackling, pulling, and sitting or lying on top of one another. It also can include hopping and rolling near one another without making contact. It might include some role playing, such as superheroes, robots, or other characters that might battle each other. It almost always includes lots of laughing.

Rick Porter (1994, 44), an early proponent of roughhousing, reminds us that this type of play is very common in children's homes: "Typically, a father, uncle, older siblings, or mother starts this by wrestling on the bed or out in the backyard with a child. . . . It starts in the family."

Roughhousing can happen indoors with a little planning. It is important to have a mat and plenty of space without toys. Unless there is a significant amount

of space, kids should roughhouse on their knees (Carlson 2011a). This allows the fall zone around the mats to be smaller. Kids should not have hard objects in the fall zone.

This is not to say that there will be no rough play in other parts of the classroom. If kids are playing superheroes or animals or other energetic play, it may involve some pushing or other contact. I find that most kids can find a way to stay in control of their bodies while playing. I define *staying in control* as moving your body without bumping into objects or people (unintentionally). This works because I don't automatically shut down the type of play, but rather remind the kids playing of our guideline ("We take care of each other"). The kids know that they can continue playing if they can remain in control. They also know that if the rough aspect is the main goal of the play, they can move to the mat and safely play in the way they want.

While this play is physical, it is not aggression. Aggression is a hostile or destructive behavior. The goal is to hurt a person physically or mentally. Aggression is very different than play. Play is a freely chosen action done for fun.

Educator Frances Carlson (2011a) suggests looking for three things to differentiate rough-and-tumble play and real fighting: facial expressions, willingness to participate, and willingness to return and extend the play. Children engage in rough-and-tumble play with those they consider friends. Children generally do not want to play with someone they see as an aggressor. If all the children involved keep moving toward the other players rather than trying to get away, it is play. Even in the game of chase, kids may run away from one another, but if they get too far away, they will slow down or even move closer.

You can also hear a difference in voices. When children are aggressive, their voices lower and they sound angry. When they are playing, their voices are higher pitched, often laughing. If they are taking on a role, the voice may be lower, but in an exaggerated, almost singsongy way to indicate that they are playing. I find that teachers who allow for roughhousing can tell the difference fairly easily. If a teacher gets nervous around any rough play, they may shut it down without looking to see if it is play or aggression.

Some children have difficulty reading social cues and/or giving social cues to let others know they are playing. A teacher who allows roughhousing provides an opportunity for these children to learn to behave respectfully toward others even when playing rough. The teacher should stay nearby and verbalize the social cues (see pages 50–51).

If a child is having a hard time controlling impulses while roughhousing with others, recognize their need to roughhouse while keeping everyone safe. If the child is young, give them a big pillow or cushion to tackle and throw around. You or another adult can also be the roughhousing partner and let them know what your boundaries are as you roughhouse. If they are older, they might prefer to throw a ball really hard or tumble on a mat.

After the child has had a chance to roughhouse, they may need help calming down. You can help them breathe deeply. They can try blowing bubbles, blowing a tissue, or lying down and putting an object on their tummy and watching it go up and down. They may want to sit in a tight space or have time alone. They may want to sit on your lap while you read a book.

Roughhousing How-To

There is more than one way to roughhouse with children. The main guideline is to always respect their needs ("We take care of each other"). If they ask you to stop or show signs of distress, by all means stop. If they didn't tell you to stop, it's a good time to remind them to verbalize their needs. If you are already comfortable roughhousing with children, you can skip this section. I will give one way to ease into it that I think works well for people who aren't entirely sure they want to roughhouse but want to meet the needs of the children.

You will want to have a mat or perhaps a few mats. If you have room, you can use mats to make a permanent big body area. You may need mats or cushions on the walls or nearby shelves as well, depending on the amount of room you have. If children are on their knees, any object more than three feet away probably does not need to be cushioned.

If you haven't allowed roughhousing in your classroom before or you have turned a blind eye to it in the past, you should start with a group time to talk about it. You could read the book *Let's Play Rough!* by Lynne Jonnell. You could also ask if anyone roughhouses (or wrestles) with their parents. Chances are many of them wrestle with a dad, an uncle, or another male family member. You can ask what it's like.

Then remind the group of your guidelines. Ask for ideas on how to roughhouse while meeting those guidelines. If you need to, you can suggest saying, "Stop" when you want someone to stop and stopping when you hear someone else say, "Stop." You could also suggest not kicking because it is hard to tell how hard you are kicking. I often suggest not grabbing necks and heads because they are more vulnerable. You may decide to limit the number of children roughhousing when you start. You may find that you can let the children regulate the number as needed once you are all comfortable with this type of play.

Once you have discussed how to meet the guidelines, you can try it out. As the children roughhouse, you should stay nearby to help facilitate the play. If someone is having trouble with cues, simply verbalize the nonverbal cues. For example, you might say, "She is scrunching up her face—she wants you to stop."

You can also model how to check in with someone if they get hurt. The injuries will probably be minor, and the child will join in play once they see that someone checked in with them. Many children will test this out when they first start playing, crying at the slightest bump to see if the others can be trusted. As the trust is built up, many children will tolerate more bumps or simply take themselves out of the play to take a break. You can verbalize these choices.

Don't stop the play completely unless a child gets hurt, a child is not easing up, or there is a true fear for safety. Remember, it is better to have a bump or bruise and learn the lesson physically than it is to have an adult tell you to stop. In the end, having children make small missteps, and learning from them is safer than having an adult prevent any and all minor injuries.

You can also act as sports announcer and give a play-by-play of what you see them doing. I find this is a great way to get kids involved. This works well for running, jumping, and other active play. Kids seem to play a little longer when I am announcing their superhero jumps.

If you decide to participate, it helps to start slowly. Go down on your knees or even on all fours. Make yourself small to start. Find out how much force they are using, and try to meet that force. Push at their shoulders with your hand or shoulder. As you get comfortable with the play, you may move on to hug-and-spill. You wrap them in your arms as if hugging them, but then drop them down on the mat. You can start by lowering them all the way to the mat and letting go (or rolling them out). Eventually, you should be able to drop them on the mat. Since you both are on your knees, they will be only a few inches from the mat.

Preschoolers and young schoolagers often take on roles such as superheroes when they are roughhousing. Rely on the children as experts who can fill you in on the names of the bad guys and the good guys and let them suggest a role for you. When you are roughhousing (or battling a superhero), you can give the children feedback on whether they are being too rough with you. You can also let them know if they can be a little rougher. I find that children with experience roughhousing will tend to be gentler with women and rougher with men, but you can let them know what is right for you.

As you roughhouse, you will get a sense of what feels right for you and the kids in your care. You may add more moves or take on roles. You may roar and growl. You may make yourself bigger. Always keep the guidelines in mind. You will find that you see the active children in a new way, and they will see you in a new way as well. A certain bonding happens with physical contact, both gentle hugs as well as wrestling.

There is usually more room when roughhousing outside, so you can allow the children to stand up. The children may want to run, chase, and tackle one another as well as roughhouse. You can help the children decide where they can do this safely and if there are any areas that should be avoided with this type of play.

Planning for Roughhousing

Call a classroom meeting (group time).

- Ask about experiences roughhousing.
- Remind everyone of guidelines.
- Brainstorm ways to meet guidelines.

Make room for roughhousing

- Use a mat to define the area.
- If desired, limit the number of children roughhousing at one time.
- Make sure everyone has a turn who wants one.
- If someone is hesitant, offer to be their roughhouse partner.
- Stay close by to support the play.

Facilitate the Play

- Check in with kids.
- Verbalize their body language.
- Mediate any potential conflicts as needed.

Warplay

As we allow children to move more and play boisterously, it is inevitable that some children will pretend to use weapons, such as guns or swords. Many teachers get uncomfortable with this type of play and shut it down as quickly as possible. This does two things: it keeps the children from playing out roles of power, and it keeps the children from deepening their play to make it richer and more complex. The story below illustrates an alternate view of what this type of play can lead to.

When I first started teaching, I would have tried to stop any warplay. I probably would have said, "We don't use guns at school." Which was usually met with, "But they're not really guns. They're Duplos." It took me awhile to learn the difference between fantasy and reality. I would have been correct in stopping preschoolers from using actual guns, but these were in fact pretend. I also had to learn the importance of fantasy play for kids. Kids need lots of fantasy where they are powerful, and the three most powerful people in our society are people

This year my classroom started with two main pretend play scenarios. There was Mom and Baby, where kids would take turns being Mom or the baby. If there were more than three kids, it was Mom and a few babies. The game involved the baby lying down for nap, cuddling, and making the bed for another nap. After a few weeks, Mom started feeding the baby as well. Caleb, Faith, and Nikita all played, but it was always "Mom" and never "Dad."

The other game was Capture the Bad Guy. This game involved the Good Guys capturing the Bad Guys, usually by shooting them, but sometimes traps were built from blocks or other things. Greg and Neville were the main players. Neville would make guns out of Duplos. Soon Greg was making Duplo guns as well. Rhett often joined in as well. Usually all three were Good Guys fighting imaginary enemies, but sometimes one of the boys would be the Bad Guy. They would point their guns at each other and make shooting sounds.

One day they were dinosaurs instead of Bad Guys, but something magical happened. Rhett became a T. rex, and he roared and held up his claws. Neville became a stegosaurus and stomped around the room. Greg flapped his arms to be a pteranodon. They each acted out their unique role and even searched for different food. Soon Neville turned into a baby T. rex and followed Rhett around the room. Not only did their play become more complex, but it actually preceded the family play in terms of having various roles for more than two people.

with guns, superheroes, and moms (Levin and Carlsson-Paige 2006). It's been almost twenty years since I started allowing warplay in my classroom, so it's hard to remember exactly what I was worried about, but I now try to see the play from the child's perspective.

One thing I have started doing recently is watching for what I call "the rules of engagement" in warplay. The rules are very set. The same is true for other pretend play, but we sometimes overlook that because this play is loud and boisterous. We often think it is chaotic or out of control, but it is usually very controlled.

In any pretend play, preschool teachers like to see children move from simple, solitary pretending to repetitive pretend play with one other child. This play may start to involve more

Mom and Baby and Capture the Bad Guy were fairly simple and repetitive games. Each one followed very specific rules. Occasionally Cora would be a baby, but she would crawl away from her parents, hoping for a chase. Caleb would never fail to let her know, "That's not how the game goes." The same thing happened when Shamus approached Greg with his own Duplo creation. Shamus held it up like a sword and knocked Greg's Duplo gun. Immediately Greg said, "No, that's not how you do it. You hold it up and go, 'Bang, bang.'" Shamus walked away, but the next day he walked up to Greg, stopped a few feet away, and pointed his gun. "Bang, bang."

than one child, but generally there are only one or two roles (everyone is pretending to be a cat, for example). By the time children start kindergarten, you would expect that most children could participate in pretend play with more than two children and more than two roles.

At this point in the year, most children were beginning to engage in this more complex pretend play, but the first ones to do it were Greg, Neville, and Rhett with their wild and loud dinosaur play. In years past, I may have spent more time trying to tone down their play (and others may have prohibited the warplay). This year I spent the time watching for the rules of engagement. This allowed me to appreciate the development of their play. I did join in occasionally, and more than once I had to intervene in a conflict, but no more than I did with those engaging in family play.

Sometimes adults can get caught up by the theme of children's play. Good Guys and Bad Guys shooting each other *is* harder to watch than Mommies and Babies going to sleep. Obviously in real life, most people would avoid an actual shoot-out. It is best to look at why children play this way. Children often take on powerful roles. Toddlers often roar like lions or dinosaurs because it feels powerful. They probably have never seen a lion roaring.

Preschoolers also like to play with power, but the roles they change are different. I like to think of these powerful roles as a continuum from nurturance to protection. The nurturance roles are things such as parents, nurses, and doctors. The protection roles can be superheroes, police, and firefighters. It is important to note that any of these roles may be played as Bad Guys. Children might choose to be the Bad Guys escaping the police, or someone might be a mom who resembles the stepmother in *Cinderella*.

I have taught workshops on warplay for early childhood teachers for almost a decade. I have had some teachers tell me that when they allowed this type of play,

they bonded with children that in the past would have remained somewhat distant. Children who witness violence, whether real or on a screen, often choose to play violent themes.

How to Appreciate Warplay

Appreciating this type of play can be a stretch for teachers who didn't engage in it as children. Like most play, I think a teacher should start with observing the play. While observing the children, figure out what the rules of engagement are. What things can the children do in their roles? What can't they do? Generally, warplay or superhero play has very set rules. Writing down these rules gives you something to do instead of stopping the play. Hopefully, learning these rules will give you some respect for the play.

Once you know the rules of the play, are there things you can do to extend the play? One year several children in my class were obsessed with pirates. A few of the children rolled up paper to make swords. I decided to have a small-group time where we tried different ways to sculpt with paper. I demonstrated a few techniques—rolling, folding, tearing, crumpling—and then let the kids work. The kids who had been rolling paper suddenly added to their skill set. They created the hilts as well as scabbards for their swords. They also started flattening the paper and curving the blades to make daggers and cutlasses. Only one child started with all of this vocabulary, but soon most of the class knew the terms.

Sometimes you can join the play. It is important not to join the play until you are ready to follow their lead. You may offer ways to expand the play, but not until the kids have had a chance to really follow their story line. Too often teachers get to this step and then suggest scenarios they are more comfortable with, such as eating dinner after saving the day. There is a time for playing Dinner, but not before there has been a lot of action. Part of the appeal of this type of play is to move quickly and be loud. Sitting at a table does not meet these needs. Finding a reason to crawl under the table might. Perhaps you could suggest going to your secret hideout and then head under the table (I can usually only fit my head and shoulders under the table, but they can fit). You may have to drive to the scene of the crime. You can set up chairs and grab a steering wheel (anything round will do). Of course whoever is driving will have to go so fast that you'll have to lean to one side when they turn and then lean to the other side when they turn again. This is a great way to engage several muscle groups, as well as address their sense of balance.

Once you have let them play boisterously for a while, you could introduce a scenario that might involve less movement or volume, such as having dinner or going home. There may be resistance. "No, there are still more bad guys." Then you need to drop your idea and follow theirs.

The other baby step you might take is in relation to aiming the guns. If you have been banning warplay (or at least attempting to), you may not be comfortable with kids pretending to shoot each other. I don't think there is anything wrong with kids pretending to shoot one another as long as all the children are okay with it. They all know it's pretend, and it can be fun to have a melodramatic death before finally falling to the ground. It is part of the game. Young children certainly don't have the same understanding of death that adults do. Even children who have witnessed shootings may be the ones who want to pretend to die, knowing they can get up again. It can be a way to feel in control of a situation in which they were powerless. At the same time, adults or other children or adults in the room who have witnessed such tragedies may have a hard time seeing this type of play even if they know it is pretend.

In either case, if your classroom is not ready for children to pretend to shoot one another, you might have them shoot at objects. Perhaps you can make targets and have a firing range (Slack and Martin 2015). You could also have toy animals and go hunting. You could have drawings of monsters (or bad guys). If the children are four or older, they could probably choose any object (e.g., a pillow or a clock) and pretend it's their target.

You may want a specific area for the gunplay so kids don't walk in the line of fire (Slack and Martin 2015). If you get comfortable with that, you could let them shoot anywhere in the room. Remember it is pretend, and all the children know it. They may still get a little upset if someone points a pretend gun at them or if someone walks into the line of fire. Conflict resolution or other problem-solving techniques should take care of this. You can still follow the same rule about targets. However, you may feel comfortable letting kids shoot at one another if they all agree.

If the children live in an area where harm could come to them if they are pretending to shoot in public, you can talk to them about where it is safe to play that way. Children in this environment may need to engage in warplay more in your classroom to feel a sense of control over something that can be quite scary for anyone, but especially a young child. These children will probably benefit from the strategies for children with high arousal (see page 38).

I do not have children use toy guns in my classroom. I think open-ended toys allow for a wider variety of play. I think the image of a gun in our society is so strong that it's hard for children to pretend it is anything else. On the other hand, any toy drill, toy hammer, or L-shaped block is going to be used as a gun at least some of the time, probably even most of the time. I can understand others using toy guns if they feel children are creative with them. Do the play themes become increasingly richer? Do the toys sometimes get used as other objects? It is admittedly hypocritical to have toy screwdrivers, drills, and hammers as well as toy stethoscopes and syringes in my classroom and claim children always need open-ended toys. I guess I would say that I have found my comfort zone, and you should find your comfort zone.

More and Less

I didn't become a teacher so I could wrestle with kids or watch them pretend to shoot one another. I loved their creativity and curiosity. I took delight in those aspects of preschoolers, while trying to stop them from roughhousing or pretending to use weapons. Over the years, I have learned to trust the children more. Now my classroom has times when the play is rougher, and the play themes can be violent, but the children themselves are more engaged. I actually spend less time redirecting and managing behavior than when I forbid roughhousing and warplay. As contrary as it sounds—much like the advice earlier that if you want children to sit quietly, you need to let them move around—you need to let them play rough if you want them to fight less.

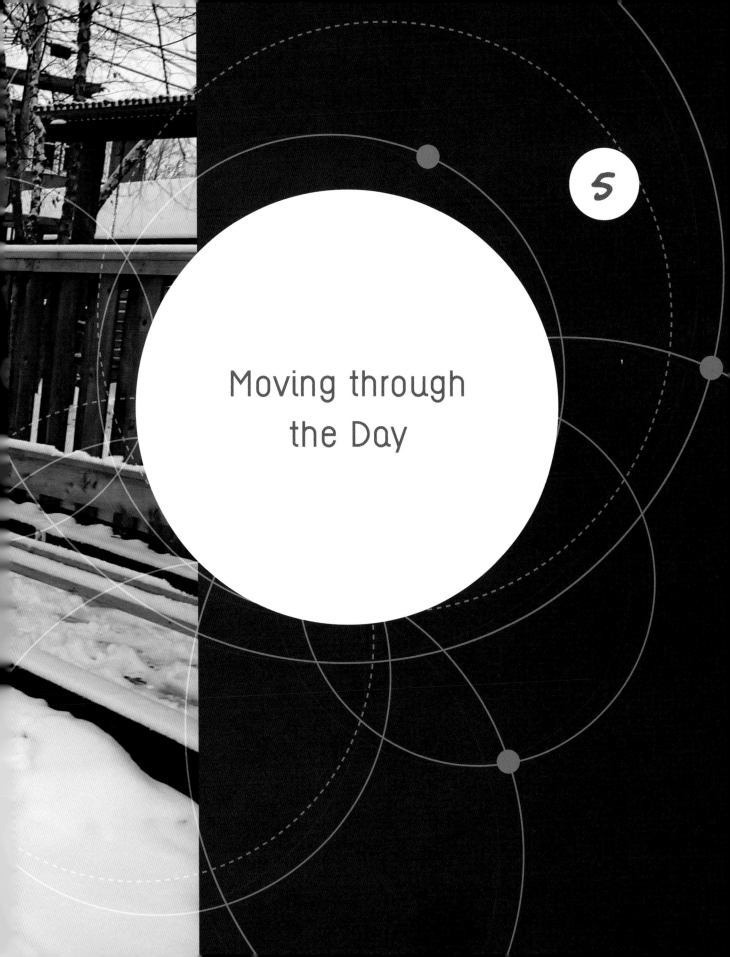

Moving through the Day

We have been looking at movement from the perspective of children and how it helps them develop in all domains. Now I want to look at our role as teachers. What do we do to help and hinder children's development? Many of us have operated under the mistaken belief that we are more effective as teachers if children are quiet so we can impart our knowledge. I certainly started teaching with this attitude. Much of my early teaching was more about order than discovery. I have found that learning requires action, and action requires movement, and the movement of young children is anything but orderly.

As I strived to make children more active in their own learning, I started slowly changing routines and expectations in my classroom. It probably took me longer than it needed to, but each change seemed to make the children more engaged and active in their own learning. The biggest change is to rethink rules and expectations. Then you can make changes to your daily routine to encourage active exploration and expression.

Rules around Bodies

Reading books to preschoolers is one of my favorite things about my job. If the classroom is getting a bit too rowdy for me, I know I can pick up a book and start reading out loud. By the time I turn to the second page, a few kids have gathered around. Soon, most of the class is sitting around me listening. I love the way kids this age become so engaged with the story that they call out when they see

One time I was at another child care center to read one of my books. As I turned the page, the illustration showed Bree holding up a worm. A child rose to his knees and pointed and said, "Look, a worm!" I was just about to say, "You're right. She does have a worm." I was thinking I could ask how many of the kids have found a worm. But I didn't say anything because a teacher scolded the child, telling him to sit quietly so I could read. I read the rest of the book, but I didn't have any other enthusiastic kids calling out.

After the book, I asked the kids questions, and they asked me some questions. The kids had a lot to say, but every time they became a bit animated (kneeling, talking over each other), a teacher scolded them. It was hard to have a conversation because the teacher kept interrupting us.

On my walk to the bus, I realized that none of the teachers commented on my books with the kids (or with me). They thanked me for reading to the kids, but otherwise the only time they spoke was to scold the children. It seemed that for the teachers the main learning experience was learning how to sit and wait for a turn to speak.

something in the illustrations or they anticipate some of the lines in the book.

Early childhood programs have many expectations around children and their bodies. Sometimes these expectations are clearly stated as rules. Sometimes the rules are spoken only when someone breaks them. Sometimes there are expectations that involve teachers stopping certain behaviors. We teachers often tell ourselves that the expectations are there to facilitate the safety of the children. The problem is,

we rarely question many of them. Any time we are telling a child to stop a certain action, we should be able to honestly explain how it endangers the child.

Many of the expectations are quite removed from any actual safety concern and may arguably be in place to facilitate learning. Again, we should always be able to explain how it facilitates learning. One example is the time-honored tradition of "crisscross applesauce." Sitting cross-legged is one way to sit that is healthy for a growing body, but it is not the only way. In fact, the only thing unhealthy about sitting cross-legged is staying in that position for long periods of time. Children should be able to choose how to sit and should move and

transition from one position to another. Sitting in one position for extended periods is the problem (Naomi Siegal, pers. comm.).

One of the reasons children should be able to move their bodies while sitting is to help them pay attention. Everyone's brain can lose focus after a while. The reticular activating system (RAS) causes the body to move, to regain focus. "The RAS activates the muscles to move in order to wake up the thinking brain and bring it back on task. In other words fidgeting can help concentration" (Connell and McCarthy 2014, 86).

The one way that children should not sit is sometimes referred to as the W position. This is when the child's legs form a W, with feet to the side and knees and buttocks resting on the floor. This position is not healthy for joint development, and, to make it worse, children tend to be anchored in the position. It's hard to move out of the position, so children don't shift to other positions as often (Naomi Siegal, pers. comm.). When I see a child in the W position, I simply ask if they can sit a different way. This usually works. I don't worry too much if a child doesn't switch positions, but I try to make sure to say something each time.

When I started teaching, I would make sure that children were looking at me before I started reading a book. I would stop reading if they were squirming too much. I did these things because I wanted everyone to listen to me. The more I understand about how our brains and bodies work together, the more I realize I probably had fewer kids listening to me this way. I should have read the book in a way that interested me, which would draw the kids in. (For more on how to read books to children, see pages 124–26).

Now when I read, I add a lot of emotion. If children are fidgeting or talking quietly, I just ignore them and keep reading. They are usually still listening, and I don't want to interrupt the flow of the story for the others. I let children sit or stand the way they want when I am reading a book. I do ask children to make sure others can see, so fairly quickly the kids and I find that the higher up you are, the further back you need to be. For example, if you want to stand, you go in back. If you want to lie down, you need to make sure no one is in front of you. I do have to remind children, but certainly no more than in classrooms where they are supposed to sit crisscross applesauce. The difference is the kids in my room can look around and see the other kids and realize why they are moving. It is not because the teacher said so, but because the child behind them is saying, "I can't see." Crisscross applesauce is about compliance; I am helping them be more aware of others.

I am not saying that teachers shouldn't have expectations for children, but rather the expectation should be focused on the goal, not on compliance. In terms of having children listen or pay attention, the goal should be to try to help children develop self-regulation. In other words, let them move their bodies to wake their brains up when needed. The great thing is that not only does it support children's development but it also lets the teacher concentrate on other things.

Moving from Rules to Guidelines

I have become more effective in reading books to children because I made a conscious effort to switch from rules to what Dan Gartrell, a professor of early childhood education, refers to as guidelines. When I had rules about how to sit during reading time, I frequently had to remind children of these rules, but eventually I got tired of saying no all the time.

I discovered what many other teachers have found. The more I try to control children, the less self-control they exhibit. When there are fewer rules, children tend to behave more prosocially when they feel in control (Marion 2014).

Guidelines go one step further because they tell children what they can do, not what they are not supposed to do (Gartrell 2012). Instead of reminding children not to hit, I remind them of our one guideline: "We take care of each other."

Guidelines also allow for gray areas that often occur. For example, we have a loft in my classroom that looks down on the classroom on three sides. Originally I had a rule that you couldn't throw things down from the loft. This was a safety issue because a block or hard toy dropped on someone's head from a few feet up could hurt someone. But situations kept coming up that called this rule into question. One time a child made a paper airplane. Throwing it from the loft didn't pose a safety issue, and it had many benefits. Think of all the spatial language we would use to describe where the plane went (over, under, through, next to, etc.). Then a few weeks later, a group of children had a pillow fight, with some throwing pillows from the loft. A few weeks later, a child watched a tissue float down from the loft. If I were honest about the rule, it would now be "No throwing things from the loft except paper airplanes, pillows, and tissues." Instead, I simply didn't say anything until a child brought it up.

When I started using guidelines, I could say, "We take care of each other, so we can't throw toys from the loft because they are hard and could hurt someone." When a child makes an airplane, I can say, "Are we still taking care of each other if you throw a paper airplane?" The child can figure out that no one will get hurt. Not only did I get rid of unnecessary rules (or having to hope that no one noticed when I ignored a rule), I am allowing the kids to practice risk assessment in a safe way.

This also brings up rules that many of us consider universal, such as "No running in the room." While running in the room in general might pose a safety concern that children may not be able to anticipate on their own, there is a lot of gray area in terms of what constitutes running. For example, is jogging okay? Isn't a five-year-old skipping more likely to result in a fall than if the same child

were jogging? Can a young child tell the difference between jogging and running? I have found myself watching children running in the room with enough control to stay safe on several occasions. I have also watched kids walking into other kids who get in their way, which probably relates more to their vestibular sense than social development. Is walking into another child a safety concern, and if so, should we ban walking in the room? I could go to that other universal rule—"No pushing"—but then what about two kids who smile as they push each other?

In the end, I am not convinced that there are universal rules, but I am convinced that there are universal guidelines. Using guidelines means that the children and I have to use our judgment when situations arise. It is good for the children to learn, and it is good practice for teachers to always reflect on their actions. Using rules can make it easy for a teacher to slip into routine.

There are other guidelines you could use, but most of them are essentially variations on the golden rule. These are a few possibilities: We are friendly with our mates. We are friendly with others. We solve problems together. Mistakes are okay, we just need to learn from them (Gartrell 2012). It's okay as long as it isn't hurting people or property (Shumaker 2012). Whatever wording you choose, it is important to post the guideline. Even though children can't actually read the words, they will know what it says. Whenever you need to remind them of the guideline, it helps to point to it to help children focus on it. Even the toddlers at our center will run over and point to the words when the teacher reminds them of our guideline.

Sitting (Or Not)

This idea of having children choose how they want to sit (or even whether to sit) changes the classroom. It requires more flexibility in the space where children meet for a group time. Children may need more space in between one another, or they may need to lean on one another.

Recently I made a small change, but it has had a big impact on how kids sit at the tables. Our freeplay is after snack. I used to stack the chairs to sweep and then put the chairs back. Now I leave them stacked up. The children are welcome to take a chair from the stack to sit in, but now the default is to stand or kneel at the table. I find that I get a wider variety of positions at the table. Once in a while, kids get a chair and sit, but more often they stand. This also results in kids moving back and forth between the table and the shelf of art supplies. More importantly, it is attracting more boys to the art area.

Even when a teacher is leading an activity, children may start by sitting at a table. For example, I start my small-group time with the kids at the table. The children sit at the same table for the start of small-group time every day. This gives them predictability. I start a brief teacher-led introduction as soon as I can before passing out materials. As the children use the materials, they might stand up or kneel on the chair. In fact, some activities require getting up.

Some schoolagers may benefit from having exercise balls to sit on. This requires the brain and body to constantly make minor adjustments to stay seated. While this can be too much for preschoolers and others who haven't made these motor controls automatic, it is a great way to keep many children actively engaged. The little adjustments actually help them pay attention.

Walking

Another time that children's bodies are heavily regulated is on walks. Of course, there are more safety concerns when leaving the center or program because you do not have control of the environment. On the other hand, you do have control over your reaction to the environment. An actual risk-benefit analysis should be done (see page 68). How likely are the threats to safety? Are there ways to minimize them? The results will vary widely. In a rural environment, preschoolers—and perhaps toddlers—may be able to run ahead to a certain landmark. In a suburban neighborhood, there may be no sidewalk, so there may be limits on walking with more freedom. Perhaps choosing routes that would allow some running or at least some other body movements might be possible.

The walk should not be thought of as a necessary task with no learning value. Rather, the walk should be considered a time for many teachable moments or, more accurately, learning moments. If teachers are planning a walk, they should consider how much time it will take and allow time for exploring or playing. If there isn't time for exploring or playing, perhaps the walk should be shorter. Just as early childhood educators emphasize the process, not the product, we should also emphasize the journey, not the destination.

When I taught in Brooklyn, New York, we did not have much of a playground of our own. Every day we would walk a block and a half to an elementary school's playground. I had children walk behind me and in front of the assistant teacher.

The children were fairly free to move about within those confines (although admittedly, I was not as tolerant of big body expression as I would be now). We would stop to notice leaves changing or other seasonal changes. The ironwork in front of each brownstone was unique, and over the year we would develop stories about the designs. We would also try hopping, walking backward, and other movements. The walk back could take awhile, and we would often arrive a half hour after the other class, but it was worth it. We were meeting lots of learning goals for preschoolers, especially relating to creativity, pretending, and literacy (with all the stories), not to mention physical goals.

After Sitting All Day

Meanwhile, after-school and other out-of-school-times (OST) programs have children who have spent several hours mostly sitting. In other words, these children need to move a lot. If the program has access to the outdoors, this can help because the children will move more when they are outside. Many in this age group also enjoy sports, so games can be organized. The trick is that the kids who don't participate in sports also need to move. Some kids may benefit from free-play on the playground, especially if roughhousing is allowed. Other children may meet these physical needs through the arts (music, dance, visual art, or theater).

It also helps if there are opportunities to move in the classroom. This can be hard for OST programs that borrow a classroom that has another use during the day. All the supplies may be on a cart, and the space is probably set up for sitting rather than physical play. A little imagination may help. You can brainstorm with the kids on how to safely meet the need for movement. Perhaps there is a hallway that can also be used. Perhaps kids can help move desks and shelves (and later move them back). Just moving shelves gives the children some movement opportunities.

The truth of the matter is that we as a society have been failing to meet the physical needs of children (and adults). Changes need to be made on many levels, but all of us can start with the things within our control. If we can add more movement to a child's time before or after school, we should take the opportunity.

Real Work

Children should also have a chance to do real work in the program. The work they do will depend on their age and abilities, of course, but they should do something. Doing work gives them a sense of agency, a sense that they can affect the environment around them. It also gives them movement experiences they might not have otherwise. The work should usually relate directly with their other experiences with your program.

It can be simple things, such as setting the table for a meal, stacking chairs, or wiping up a spill. If you have pets, children can help care for the animals. You can also have them do seasonal tasks, such as raking leaves, shoveling snow, and

weeding gardens. All of these tasks involve several hand motions, bending, lifting, and other movements both large and small. Of course, children may not be able to do a thorough job, but they should feel they are contributing. We have a snow removal service, but I always make sure we get out early and push a few square feet of snow off the sidewalk. At pickup time, many of the children will let their parents know that our class is responsible for the clear sidewalks.

I would encourage you to serve meals family style for preschoolers and schoolagers if your state's regulations allow it. Preschoolers can be moderately challenged by serving spoons, tongs, and pitchers. Remember that these movements won't be automated at first. The children may not be able to talk to you while pouring. Try not to engage them in conversation while they are pouring, or they may end up spilling. Of course, even if they are focused on the task, they may spill a bit but remain calm. Now they can practice their cleanup skills as well. If you have laundry in your program, you can simply have rags on hand. I also like to use a small squeegee for milk or water spills. Children actually gain these skills much faster when they can practice daily, so in the long run there will probably be fewer spills.

Daily Schedule

Many aspects of my daily schedule also changed as I allowed more freedom of movement. You will probably find yourself changing some things as well. I have listed various activities from a typical full-day program. Daily schedules vary widely depending on the program. An after-school program is going to be much different than a full-day family child care program. On the other hand, all programs benefit from having a consistent schedule. Children feel more secure when they know what to expect. A consistent schedule can also help children self-regulate by offering times with more sen-

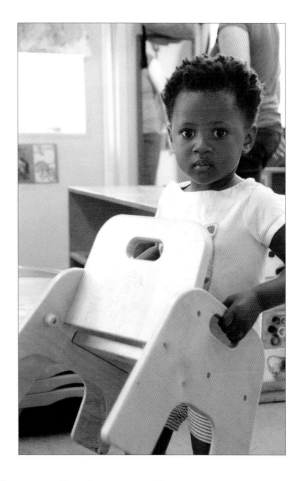

sory stimulation and other times with less stimulation to allow for recovery. In fact, if you have a child who has a hard time regulating, you may need to adjust your schedule.

A schedule needs to allow times for children to amp up and play vigorously followed by quieter times for them to recover. There should be times where the whole group is together and times when children choose their activities. If a program is only a portion of the day, you should take into account what the rest of the day is like for the children. For example, most kids come to an after-school program after spending much of the day sitting. These children should spend most of their time moving. On the other hand, a religious education class is usually shorter, and children will probably have time to play physically afterward. These children (especially older children) may spend most of the time in conversation.

Children should not have to wait long to move their bodies. Infants should have tummy time. The duration will vary depending on the age of the infant, about five minutes two or three times per day for a newborn, gradually increasing both duration and frequency. Toddlers should be able to freely move their bodies throughout the whole day except for nap, meals, time in cars or bikes, and diapering. Preschoolers will have group times when they should stay in the same area, and their movements should not be disruptive. Except for naptime, they should not have to wait more than a half hour to move around. Instead, find ways to allow them to move during all parts of the schedules. Schoolagers should not have to sit for more than two hours, preferably much less than that.

It is also important to schedule time for you and the other teachers to reflect and plan. This may include planning specific activities, but you should also take the time to reflect on your environment, materials, and schedule. Does anything need to change to better meet the needs of all the children? We are usually good at meeting the needs of most of the children, but we often struggle with one or two, either because they are the quiet child we don't focus on as often as others, or they are the boisterous child. Taking the time to reflect and plan every day— even if it is only five minutes—can help us reach *all* the children.

The following times listed for a schedule won't pertain to every program; however, there are a few basics to keep in mind. For example, having a group time near the beginning of the day can help build a sense of belonging. Full-day programs should have a quieter time for young children to rest both physically and mentally.

Group Times

There are several types of group times, such as circle time, small-group time, calendar, message board, and movement time. The group may be the entire class, or it may be split up into smaller groups, each with one teacher. What they have in common is that they are teacher initiated and teacher directed, although they often include input from the children. These times should generally be shorter than the child-initiated times of the day. The goal is to have group time be long enough that children have time to engage and feel part of the activity but not too long that some children lose interest. If a group time involves mostly talking, fidgets can keep children focused (see page 108).

Greeting Time/Calendar

This time may be a separate part of the daily routine, or it may be part of circle time. I am referring to times when the whole class is meeting near the beginning of the day and mostly talking. They may look at a calendar, message board, weather chart, or something else.

One time I was going over our message board with the class. Ivan had been dropped off a few minutes earlier and wanted to be alone. He went in the book area. It was located on the other side of the room, but he could see me and the message board. I was reading a message that Jalia, a four-year-old, asked me to write. The day before, the two of us had taken photographs of road signs and taped them to cardboard. After several attempts, we figured out how to make these signs stand up to be used with our toy cars.

Just as I started to read the message, Ivan started talking to me. He was still a little bit sad from drop-off. I was the only adult in the classroom, so I told the kids I would be right back. I went over to Ivan with the intention of having him sit in my lap so I could comfort him while talking to the whole class. Before I even got to the book area, however, Jalia picked up one of the signs we had made. She started to explain how she made them and passed around several of the signs for the other children to see firsthand.

I paused and let her talk for a few minutes until it seemed like she was done. Then I took over to read the next message. The other children were engaged, asking Jalia questions, handling the signs, and passing them around. Ivan and I joined the group after a few minutes. The children had always been active participants when reviewing our message board. On this day, they were able to continue the discussion without input from me or any other teacher.

Keep time spent talking as brief as necessary. Don't shortchange the depth of conversation, however. If there is discussion, the teacher should find ways to include as many voices as possible. When one child makes a point, the teacher could ask the class for their reaction. In other words, let them voice their opinions. Use open-ended questions. You can build off the answers, making connections to previous conversations or comments from other children. Eventually you may be able to let the children lead the conversation and only jump in if it stalls.

If only a few children are still engaged in the conversation, you may need to pause and continue the conversation later. You can talk more in smaller groups, at mealtimes, or even one-on-one when the opportunity arises. Also, if a child or two seem to lack basic background information about a topic of discussion, try to talk to them individually, read books, or provide experiences that can give them a better understanding of the topic.

Walking Meeting

Another idea that I have found helpful is the walking meeting. I learned this from the corporate world. This works well for brainstorming when creativity is the key. I used to brainstorm with the class sitting down as a group to plan a final event for our investigations. We would sit and talk. I could usually get through about ten minutes at the most before most of the class would lose interest. There would always be one or two kids who could keep talking. I would try to talk to those kids (and others) during mealtimes to get more ideas. Then we would sit and brainstorm as a group later in the day. It would take two or three of these group sessions to plan our finale.

Then I read about walking meetings where coworkers hold meetings while walking together. Walking meetings are used by many tech companies and have been found to encourage creative thinking. I grabbed a clipboard and went on a

walk with the class. Our center is in the city, so we had natural stopping points at each corner as we went around the block. We stopped at the first corner and talked for a while. I took notes. When interest seemed to be waning, we walked to the next corner. By the time we went around the block, we had our plan.

Two things helped. First, I think walking and being outside helped kids focus, and second, when some kids lost focus, they could squirm, talk to a friend, or lie down without interrupting those who were still engaged. I find that kids will go in and out of being engaged. If we did this inside, the kids who were squirming would eventually distract others and cause them to lose focus.

Artifacts/Projector or Smart Board

Another way to keep children engaged in a group time conversation is to have visuals. You could have artifacts or concrete samples of whatever you are talking about. One time when we were talking about tools, I passed around hammers, screwdrivers, and drills. As we talked, children could describe the tools or make connections between the tools themselves and our conversation. Children who have a harder time following a conversation could focus more on the tools.

You can use a projector or smart board to make images larger. Children seem to engage more actively with bigger images. They may run around, jump up and down, or simply point as they talk. I have been using a pico (or handheld) projector lately because it can work with batteries, so there's more flexibility in the space. I find it works well with toddlers. I simply project photographs from a walk earlier in the day, and the kids start verbally describing the walk. I used the projector recently when a storm prevented us from going out to draw some road signs. We had plenty of photographs of signs, so we projected them on a wall and drew those.

Movement Time/Music Time

Other group times also involve doing music or movement with children. They could include finger plays, full body movement, playing instruments, or singing. You can teach the children different creative movements, or children can come up with their own ideas. Some teachers use video to record children's movements and then have them try to mimic their own movements at a later time.

You can also use this time to teach movement skills and concepts rather than creative movement to music. At the end of our morning outside time, we meet by our hill on the playground. We spend about five minutes trying a movement skill. I usually demonstrate it briefly and let them try it out. I focus on skills that children learn best when guided by an adult (as opposed to learning on their own in play), such as galloping, skipping, balancing, and dribbling (Epstein 2014).

Transitions

Transitions between activities can often be stressful for teachers. We have a specific goal in mind, such as getting all the children to the playground. Children, on the other hand, don't necessarily have the same goal in mind. Usually they want to continue playing or socializing with friends. I find it is easy to get focused on my goal and forget to consider the perspective of the children. When I am at my best, I find that transitions can meet the needs of the children, allowing them to play or socialize while still getting to where we needed to go. This is often achieved by allowing the children to move their bodies in fun ways. Children don't need to move through hallways in a line. If there are two teachers, you could ask the children to walk between the two of you. If other classes might be disturbed by noise, you can ask children to be quiet or even ask them to "sneak" through without the other teachers hearing them. You could also have them move in other ways. They could crawl or scoot down the hallway. They could follow the way you move.

If they are moving to a new activity within the classroom, try to avoid long wait times. Is there something they could do while the others are getting ready? If we simply expect children to wait, we should expect them to fidget. They may also make physical contact with friends, such as leaning, pushing, and so on. This should be expected, especially among preschoolers and young schoolagers. They are not purposely breaking rules; they are simply doing what children do at this age—move constantly.

My class has to walk about twenty feet from our playground to the front door of our school. Before opening the gate, I always say, "You can run down the ramp or walk to the door, but no sneezing." Most kids run down the ramp yelling, "Ahh-choo!" I tell them not to sneeze because they are so focused on breaking this (silly) rule that they don't push or tease each other about being faster than others. They are in on the same joke.

Like every other time of day, we need to give children something to do with their bodies, or they will figure out something on their own. While I do give children something to do for most transitions, there are times when I don't. I used to worry about this, but now I find it is a great time to let the kids figure it out on their own. They might get a little loud, and they might get a little physical. But now I have learned just to take a deep breath and let them be kids.

Freeplay/Work Time (Including Arrival and Departure)

Freeplay in my room can look a little different than it used to before I allowed more freedom of movement. Sometimes people will come into my classroom and see six kids roughhousing on the mat while other kids are painting at the easel, usually also painting their arms as much as the paper. It can seem loud and maybe chaotic if you are not used to it, but the kids are engaged. Ten minutes later, the same kids are often sitting on the floor building with Mobilos, teaching one another new ways to make their creations move. The others are washing off their arms and the floor. People often comment on how focused the kids are.

I think the kids in both examples are focused, but in different ways. We often dismiss loud physical play as unfocused and chaotic, but it can be very purposeful. Joey Schoen of the Dodge Nature Preschool in Saint Paul, Minnesota, put it this way: "Whenever someone tells me that boys don't pay attention, I always say, 'Have you tried giving them a shovel and a pile of dirt? They usually pay attention for at least a half hour.'" I want all children to be engaged and focused on something during freeplay in my classroom. To do that, I need to make a variety of toys and activities available so that kids can engage their whole bodies or sit quietly in groups of several children or alone. (For more on how to set up the environment, see chapter 6.)

The children in these examples needed time to have their play scenarios combine. Some kids can take fifteen minutes just to settle into an activity. Having forty-five minutes to an hour for freeplay allows children to deepen their play, making it more complex. Even with this amount of time, children may want

Lesley, Aretha, and Carolyn were princesses. They were sitting on hollow blocks that they were pretending were their thrones. Their thrones were tucked in a small alcove separated from the rest of the room by a low wall. They sat and talked about being princesses. Aretha thought they needed wands, so she went to make one in the art area.

Just on the other side of the wall, Mark, Johan, and Bryan were playing Star Wars. None of them had seen any of the movies, but they knew Darth Vader was the bad guy and Luke Skywalker and Han Solo were the good guys. They were sitting on the floor pretending to fly a spaceship. Soon they were arguing over who was Luke and Han. No one wanted to be Darth Vader, but they didn't know any other characters.

Lesley, who had an older brother who loved the movies, knew quite a bit about Star Wars. She told them that she was Princess Leia and that Mark could be Chewbacca. The boys perked up. Lesley said she could take them to the Death Star to get Darth Vader. She told Carolyn she was Queen Amidala. The five of them played together for the next twenty minutes, the boys occasionally jumping ship to fight off Darth Vader, and the two girls still sitting on the blocks. Aretha worked alone and focused in the art area the entire time. It took time, but all of these children found ways to play that allowed for different levels of movement and different levels of interaction.

to play longer or continue building. If at all possible, allow children to save the things they are working on. Ideally, the children could save block buildings and other things on the floor. You may only be able to have them save smaller things that can be put on a shelf. Children could revisit their creations later in the day or the next day. This also makes it easier for children to stop playing and move on to a new activity. If you really can't save things, perhaps you could take pictures of them (either drawing or photographing them). This would at least give children a visual reminder of where they left off.

Mealtimes

Mealtimes are important if children are going to move their bodies. Children need to be well nourished. You can teach them about nutrition during mealtimes with simple, short sentences (think of a tweet rather than a lecture). Toddlers can learn that certain foods are everyday foods or healthy foods, and other foods are sometimes foods or a treat. Preschoolers can start to learn about food groups and even some basics, such as how grains provide energy, vegetables keep you healthy, and beans and meat make you strong. Older preschoolers and schoolagers can learn vocabulary, such as *carbohydrates*, *protein*, *vitamins*, and the like. The important thing is to spend a short time on this so that children don't get bored. One or two sentences a day should be enough. If anyone wants to know more, they will ask.

Mealtimes should be relaxed so that informal conversations can happen. Mealtimes are a time to get to know one another in most cultures, and it is a time to talk and to listen. Infants are usually interacting one-on-one with an adult during mealtimes. Toddlers and young preschoolers often talk to an adult even if there are other children around. Older preschoolers and schoolagers talk to one another. Many children learn to join a conversation through observation and trial and error. Some children will need a little extra help. It is most effective to

give short but direct instructions, such as "Say her name and then start talking." Some children try to wait until the other child verbally responds to their name before talking again. Other times children will make eye contact but not start talking. Each case will be different. The important thing is to keep the direct instruction very brief.

Children should have calm bodies while they eat to reduce the risk of choking. Whether children sit while eating is dictated more by culture than anything else. In terms of safety, children can walk or stand while they eat. This can help some children eat more at mealtime.

Children use a lot of motor skills when they eat. You can help children develop these skills. You can have them gradually serve themselves. This can involve spooning, using tongs, pouring, twisting, and more. You can challenge them to gain a little more independence, taking small steps frequently.

Book Time

Reading books can really help focus children. Books can also energize children, getting them excited. Both of these reactions are important, and both should be encouraged at some point each day. The way you read and allow children to interact will depend on whether you are trying to amp them up or wind them down.

Amping Up with Books

It is important to read books to get children excited. This may mean reading fiction that kids can act out. It could also be nonfiction that introduces a topic for further investigation. Often this type of reading (to generate excitement) happens during other parts of the daily routine, such as freeplay, when you can read to an individual child or a small group. It may also happen at group time when you may act out a story or start an investigation.

You can read fiction to excite children one-on-one, in a small group, or as a larger group. You can get them to read along with you or finish sentences by pausing. You can also have them act out the book. I like to read a story once sitting and then carry it around with me as we act out the book. If there are different settings in the book, we find different areas of the room to represent those settings. Again, it is important to alter your tone of voice. Find places to get loud and get quiet. You might change your voice. You can use the book as a prop to demonstrate an action in the book. If a character falls in the book, for example, you can slap the book down on your lap as you read the words. If a character flies, you can raise the book in the air.

Winding Down with Books

At times when you want to have children try to settle their bodies and wind down, books can help. Many children have bedtime routines that include reading books with a parent or guardian. Reading with them can be a very intimate time that stirs up warm feelings. However, if the reading lasts too long, it can also make children squirmy. This can be especially tricky if you are reading to a group of children with varying interest in the book (or reading in general).

Here are a few things that may help keep the children's interest without revving up the room: Keep noise to a minimum, but do not expect absolute silence. Read at a comfortable volume and make sure it is quiet enough that kids will need to focus to hear. If children start getting louder, try reading a little more quietly. Sometimes the children making the noise will quiet down to hear you. Other times, other children will say they can't hear. Then you can ask everyone to be quiet enough to allow everyone to hear the book ("We take care of each other").

Ask "wonder" questions at the end of a page, such as "I wonder what will happen next." "How do you think they will solve this problem?" If the children are familiar with the book, you can ask what they remember. "Do you remember what happens to them?" This should be done in moderation so you don't lose the momentum of the story, but it can really get kids engaged so their attention doesn't wander elsewhere for too long. This can be another way to get the focus back on the story if it gets too loud, although you should not do it in a negative way (such as questioning a child who may not have been listening). Rather, ask a question that will genuinely make kids want to answer.

Kids will often want to call out responses to the book or get up and point. This is a sign that they are interested, so you do not want to totally shut this down. Try to respond in an even tone to show that you hear them and understand they are interested. If several kids want to do this and you are worried about losing momentum, acknowledge that they have a lot to share and ask them to tell you more after the book ends because you really want to see what happens next. In other words, try to match their enthusiasm, rather than trying to temper it. If other teachers are sitting with the kids, they can whisper to kids to acknowledge their responses while you continue reading.

You can also offer children fidgets to use during the book reading. Fidgets are small toys that children can manipulate while listening to the book. Some children may make noises or voices as they play with the fidgets. Again, you can remind them that we have to be quiet enough so that everyone can hear the story.

Whenever reading a book, you should modulate your voice, slowing down sometimes, raising and lowering your volume. When you are reading to wind down, you might not read quite so loud, but you can use a whisper-shout (whisper with the tone and timbre of a shout). The point is to create drama. Many good picture books have a page break in the middle of a sentence. This is a time to raise your pitch and then pause before turning the page.

Having children join you on certain lines, especially repeating phrases in the book, is always a good idea. They can make sounds or say the words along with you. It may seem that you should only have them do this in a quieter way when you are reading to wind down, but that is not always the case. It is okay to have children roar or make loud sounds. This can actually release some tension or energy. This is especially good before naptime so that they are less likely to release that energy after the lights go out. If you let children roar in the middle of a book, you can end the story with a whisper.

Naptime

Children five and under in full-day programs will need to nap. This means they will need to wind down, which happens gradually. Have a quiet activity immediately before they are expected to lie down. Giving them opportunities to amp up earlier in the day is just as important.

After lunch in my classroom, children can sit and draw on one side of the room or they can pillow fight on the other side while others finish up (and I clean up). After that we read books before having naptime. I allow children to help bring out the cots. Once they are lying down on the cots, I tell a story. Finally, I come around and talk to each child one-on-one and give back rubs.

When I first allowed pillow fighting before naptime, I worried that kids would have a hard time settling down, but I was pleased to find just the opposite. The active kids were much quieter during book time and naptime. I have also found that having kids move the cots gives them heavy work, which can help them self-regulate. After nap, we go back outside to amp up the kids again, and the cycle starts over.

These are ways we can help children explore more and express themselves freely. As I have made these changes, my classroom has become less uniform but not chaotic. Children are much more in control of themselves, and they get along better with others. I don't necessarily teach less, but I spend less time restricting children and more time asking about their discoveries.

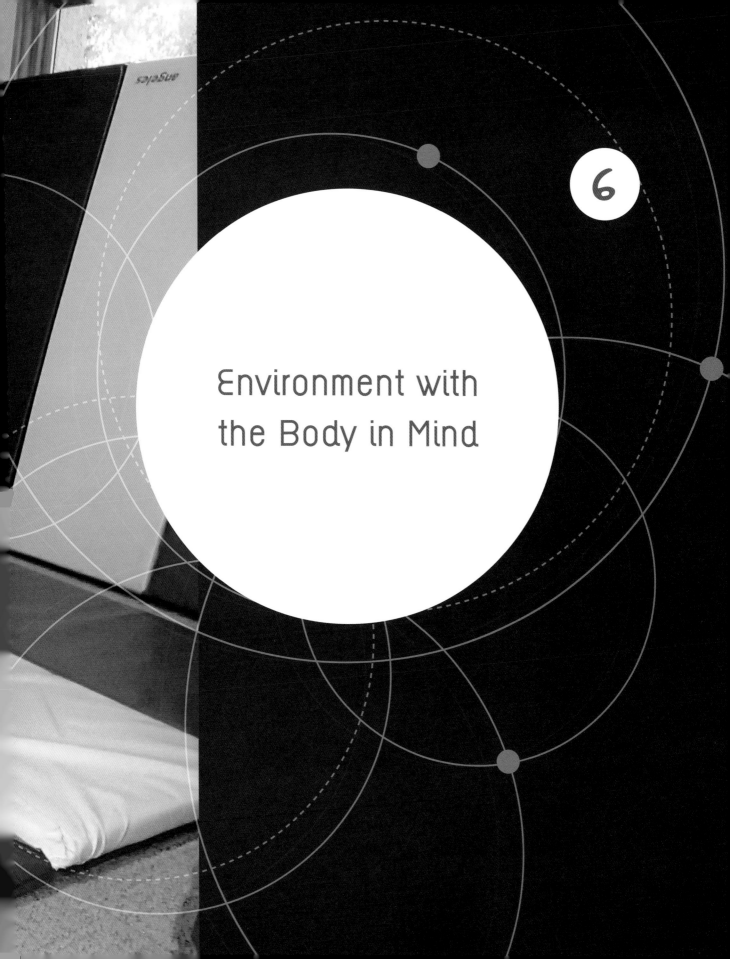

Environment with the Body in Mind

6

As I allowed children more freedom to explore and express themselves, I had to rethink my classroom environment. You will probably have to make some changes as well. Some parts of the environment we can't change, but we can change our attitude toward it. For example, if there is an entryway that is owned by the church you rent from, you might not be able to get rid of the railing that is wide enough for children to climb on. You could brainstorm with the children how to climb as safely as possible on the railing instead, or if it's not strong enough, brainstorm what you could climb on when waiting in the entryway or soon after. Again, I am not advocating a free-for-all, but if multiple children display the same behavior or the same child consistently demonstrates the same behavior, it is our job as teachers to meet that need.

When I switched to guidelines and started allowing big body play throughout much of the day, I found my old room arrangement of my preschool classroom lacking. I had arranged the interest areas to dissuade kids from moving around the room, and for the most part encouraged kids to sit down much of the time. There are good reasons to have interest areas in an early childhood classroom. The design helps children to naturally divide into smaller groups, which

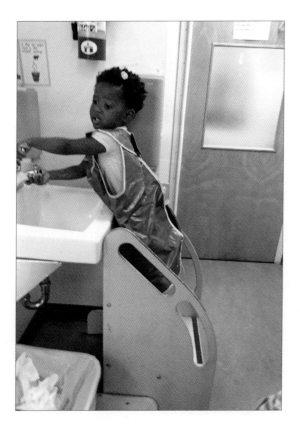

is easier for each child to navigate (both in terms of sensory processing and social skills). It is also easier for me to interact with children on a one-on-one basis or in a smaller group. In a sense, the classroom arrangement becomes another teacher. It helps guide children into engaging play as well as inspires a sense of wonder and exploration.

This division of the room makes sense. It would be hard for most kids to negotiate space if they were all in the midst of a large open room with materials on the sides. Some activities, such as drawing, take up a relatively small amount of room but require dedicated floor space (so that no one walks on the drawing). Other activities, such as block building, require more space and lots of walking back and forth because the materials are big and bulky. Pretend play can take up even more room and can often move from one location to another as the scenario changes.

It also makes sense to have the room divided with areas that have more space and less space, areas that can comfortably hold all the children in the class and areas that comfortably hold one or two. Some spaces may have harder surfaces so that messy play or artistic activity can happen. The harder surfaces facilitate easier cleanup, as well as provide stability, keeping paper in place to allow markers and pencils to work as the child intends. Some spaces should have softer surfaces to make things cozy and accommodate leaning, cuddling, and lying down. Softer surfaces also can accommodate big body play.

Children should have a sense of ownership of their environment. To do this, they need independence, which requires knowing where materials are stored. If children have an idea, they should be able to find the materials fairly easily, usually without a teacher's help, and they should know how to put them away so they can be found again.

Of course, these skills are learned and require some teacher guidance, but the goal should be independence. When a child says, "I need a marker," the teacher should ask, "Where would you find a marker?" If the child doesn't know, of course the teacher can show them and comment on the area where the markers are and finally where on the shelf they belong. Eventually the child will remember and go to the shelf. In the next stage, the child will go without asking.

Interest areas should be a starting point, not an end point. The emphasis should be on what experiences we want children to have, realizing that children may have very different ideas than the ones we planned. The interest areas will help organize materials, and a child may start in that area, but exploration and curiosity are often bigger than one interest area. Children will often need to bring materials to other interest areas.

There may be a concern that the classroom will get too messy if children are allowed to bring materials from one area to the other. A few tactics may help. For example, teachers can require children to put away materials when they are done with them before moving onto other materials. This is no more work than policing materials as children try to cross interest area borders with contraband. I personally temper this with how engaged children are. If a child is very busy in the dramatic play area but has left a few Legos in the book area, I will probably clean them up without saying anything, setting the stage for another child

to use the book area. If the child left the Legos and is wandering from interest area to interest area, I may ask them to clean up and then ask them if they have a plan for what to do next.

Sometimes teachers also worry about how many children are in an interest area. If a lot of children are trying to play or explore in a certain area, something is working! The last thing you should do is try to stop it. Instead, figure out ways to have children get their needs met while taking care of each other. They are already showing us what they are inspired by; now we have to encourage that. On top of that, you can have children practice their problem-solving skills as they come up with solutions. It helps that they are motivated to work toward a solution.

Guidelines and conflict resolution can be used to solve any potential problems. If an area is getting too crowded, help the children think of ways to allow room for everyone. If the book area is crowded, where are other comfortable places to read? If the block area is getting full, can the buildings extend into other areas? Some of this means teachers need to plan for flexibility. Can sensory materials be added to tubs at the art table? You may have an increase in conflicts at first, but children will become better problem solvers and will soon solve many of these conflicts on their own.

There can be real safety concerns with activities such as woodworking. You can't have kids crowding around a workbench swinging hammers. This can be limited by requiring goggles at the workbench and providing only the number of goggles to match the number of children that the space can accommodate. This may be the case for a big body play area as well, depending on your space. You may need to find a way to limit the number of kids. Perhaps some kids can be the audience, cheering on two kids roughhousing as in the story of the program that has Let's Go Wild time (page 45).

Remember that the interest areas may change throughout the year, maybe because students are interested in a certain material. Or maybe you need to accommodate the physical needs of a particular child or children, such as making room for a child using a wheelchair. You might also need to make room for a child who needs more personal space. No matter what the needs are or the type of play that is happening, remember the whole child—not just their eyes if they are reading, not just their hands if they are building. All areas need to be designed with the body in mind.

Quiet and Loud Areas

Every child needs the chance to move their whole body and play boisterously, but they also need places to look at books or draw quietly. It is important for all teachers to have a variety of environments in their classrooms. Areas that might facilitate more boisterous play, such as dress-up, sensory stations, big body, or art areas, should be open most of the time. Children shouldn't have to wait to move their bodies.

Sometimes a quiet area, such as a book area, might be used by children playing boisterously. One teacher told me a story about two children who brought a small football into the book area and jumped on the pillows. They would toss the ball to each other and jump on each other and roll on the pillows.

One way to look at this situation is to see two children misbehaving by playing rough (and loud) in a quiet area. Another way to consider it is that these children saw an area that was not being used and was enclosed, so they could play boisterously without disturbing someone else. The children were using good judgment and thinking about how their personal actions could affect others.

I used to reserve certain areas as quiet areas, but I have let go of this. Now that we have the guideline "We take care of each other," children can use their own judgment. If they are loud and it is not affecting the other children negatively, I don't worry about it. It also means I have to make sure children still have places to be quiet, and I can help any child who seems to be looking for a quiet space to find one; that is, help them use their judgment.

This is not to say that a book area can't be designed as a quiet area. And children should not barge in on a child reading quietly. But if no one else is using the

I was renovating my book area in my classroom. It's small, no room for a chair. But that was okay. I wanted to make it cozy. I put a cushion along the wall with matching pillows. I pictured children sitting together or with an adult, leaning on the pillows or each other and looking at books in a quiet and peaceful setting. I knew this was a great way for children to bond with one another or with a teacher.

Within a few minutes, Nate picked up a pillow and threw it at Calvin. Soon they were both tossing pillows back and forth. I had to forget about my intentions and observe the intentions of the children. I could become disappointed that I failed, or I could open my eyes and see that they were bonding. It might not be a book. It might not be quiet. But with each bop of a pillow, they were creating bonds that are the building blocks of friendship.

Petra was playing at the sensory station with Quentin and Tou. She was pretending the apparatus was a candy factory. Tou called it a "chocolate factory," and Petra burst into tears. She walked away saying, "It's not a chocolate factory. It's a candy factory." She squeezed into her cubby. Her shoulders scrunched together as she sat down. She quickly caught her breath and stopped crying. A minute later, Quentin came over and said, "We have to deliver the candy. Can you help?" Petra jumped up and said, "Okay, but it's not chocolate candy; it's hard candy." She joined Quentin and Tou back at the sensory station. The pressure from the sides of her cubby helped her regulate her body and calm down so she could play.

area, children playing boisterously may correctly see it as an enclosed place that could keep their play from interrupting the play of others.

If I am going to view big body play as important, I need to be open to it happening in multiple areas. I would not stop a child from using a ramp in the block area because inclined planes are a simple machine and belong in the science area. I wouldn't stop a child from writing a menu in the dramatic play area because it should be done in the writing area. If anything, I want to encourage this cross-domain learning.

One last point about quiet areas: Children need a variety of quiet areas. Some children like a small area with pillows, blankets, stuffed animals, or other soft materials. Other children may want a tight spot where they can feel pressure, such as between a couch and the wall, a cubby, or other tight area. Still other children may want to be in an open area where they can watch other children at play. These are all ways of being quiet and should be accommodated. The truth is, if there is a space, children will fill it.

Messy Areas

I have stated that children should be allowed to move materials from one area to another, but there are limits. Certain materials are messy and may be hard to clean in some areas and could cause a slight risk (such as slipping). Paint, clay, and most materials from a sensory table fit into this category. There may be other materials in your classroom of this type as well.

Again, the guideline about taking care of each other can include not wrecking things that belong to others. Keeping paint or crayons away from furniture or other toys shows respect for those belongings. Sensory materials could present a risk for slipping, so the same guideline can be invoked.

Every teacher has a different level of tolerance when it comes to mess. There is also a difference between a classroom that is shared with other programs (such as an after-school program), rooms in the provider's home (as in family child care), and a classroom that is dedicated to one group of children. This does not mean that these programs don't have activities that might be messy, but they may need to be more deliberate in planning how to contain the mess or how to clean it up.

But making a mess is an important part of play. Children seem to feel powerful when they make a mess. Gill Connell refers to this as a child's "dramatic expression" of the "power to do things herself" (Connell and McCarthy 2014, 81).

You should have extra clothes on hand. Depending on the families' comfort level, you may use the extra clothes to change into after the messy activity, or you may change before the activity so the clothes from home do not get messy.

You should also have plastic bags on hand to bag up messy clothes or towels and such. A clothesline can be used to dry clothes as well. A hair dryer is handy for children who can't tolerate wet sleeves. Not only will it dry the sleeve quickly, but the child will also feel a sense of responsibility as they wave the dryer over the wet spot (and probably on their face at one point as well).

Involving children in cleanup can instill a sense of belonging and efficacy. Children feel like the room is their shared responsibility. Meanwhile they are getting lots of practice with motor skills, and they experience cause and effect as the room changes. Children can use hand brooms with dustpans, rags, and towels. Cleanup may take a little longer (and you may have to finish without the children), but the children will be involved, so the teacher's attention isn't split by the cleanup and supervision of the children. It is okay if some children aren't involved, but if someone needs closer supervision, they can work with you and the other helpers. In mixed-age groups, the teacher can give different tasks depending on ability. For example, the older kids may use wet rags and the younger ones may use dry rags.

Sensory Station (Table) with Dry Materials

You can surround a sensory station, whether it includes one table, multiple tables, ramps, tubes, or something else, with carpet runners. Carpet runners are narrow pieces of carpet and can be purchased fairly inexpensively. They are usually two or three feet wide and come in a variety of lengths. It is also possible to have a small carpet that covers the whole area. The carpeting keeps loose material

from being tracked into the rest of the room. When it is time for cleanup, you can sweep the carpet, pour the debris into a pile (or directly in the trash), or simply roll the carpet up to deal with later. You can also sweep material under the table to be dealt with later.

It also helps to have shelves blocking off the area so materials don't spill into other areas or walkways. Hollow blocks or even cardboard boxes can also create a barrier for loose materials.

Sensory Station with Wet Materials

Preparing for wet materials will be different depending on whether the materials can potentially cause stains. If you are just using water, and water won't harm the floor, you don't need to cover the floor. I have found the easiest way to deal with liquid materials is to use towels to dry the floor as the play is happening and immediately after. You can buy towels fairly inexpensively at used clothing stores. The towels can later be cleaned in the laundry. Children can also use the towels to help clean up. Towels work well for cleaning up other household materials, such as cornstarch or shaving cream. I don't like to use mops because they tend to leave the floor wet and need to be cleaned and disinfected after use.

You probably want the floor covered if you are using paint or other materials that could stain. Tarps are an easy way to cover a big area. Single-use plastic paint tarps can be used, but they tear easily. Tarps may be a bit more expensive, but they last for years. Tarps can be folded up and cleaned later, or you can let the paint dry and leave it on. You may need to tape the edges to the floor or otherwise secure them.

Vinyl tablecloths can be used on top of tables and folded up for later cleaning. They last for several months on tabletops, but they don't last long on the floor. Shower curtains also work well. Children can use rags and old towels to wipe up messes. Have a bucket of soapy water on hand to help with this.

Depending on the age of the children, you can wring out the rags, or you can leave the bucket on the floor and let them do it. Be prepared with a few more towels to wipe up the excess water from cleanup. It may seem more chaotic and messy, but I find it is actually quicker to have kids help wipe up even if I have to do a last wipe down with a dry towel.

Type of sensory material	What to have on hand	Quick cleanup	Final cleanup
Dry materials	Carpet runners	Roll up carpet runner.	Clean carpet runners.
	Broom	Sweep rest under table.	Have children help sweep up material.
Water-based materials	Carpet runners or tarp	Roll up carpet runner.	Kids change clothes if needed.
	Towels/big rags	Give each child a rag.	
	Extra clothes for kids		Use hair dryer for kids who don't like the feeling of wet sleeves.
	Hair dryer		
Paint	Tarps	Roll up the tarp, tablecloth, or shower curtain.	Kids change clothes if needed.
	Vinyl tablecloths		
	Shower curtain	Kids wash with small rags.	Use hair dryer for kids who don't like the feeling of wet sleeves.
	Bucket of soapy water	Dry with towels.	
	Small rags		Clean tarp or let dry.
	Towels/big rags		
	Extra clothes for kids		
	Hair dryer		

Art Area

The art area is a place where children can express themselves through visual media. The art area in a typical program tends to attract children who enjoy sitting down for longer periods of time. More active learners usually express themselves visually with block structures and things they make with Legos, Magna-Tiles, and other manipulatives. These are great ways to express ourselves, but the use of art materials allows us to create something that can be saved and

reflected on later. In my classroom, some children bring home a dozen drawings a day for their parents, while others don't bring home anything because their creations were made of blocks that have been put back on the shelf. The latter miss the opportunity to show their parents their work, and without the object in front of them, many young children are unable to recall much about their creation. They may say that they built a spaceship but are unlikely to describe any details.

You can encourage more artwork from the block builders in your classroom with a few changes. These changes may also entice the children who stick to markers on paper to try other materials.

Stock the area with art supplies—markers, crayons, colored pencils, paint. Stock a variety of sizes of paper, including child-size paper (four feet or more). Depending on your classroom, you may offer the big paper only occasionally or on request (make sure they see it at least once a week, or they won't request it). If possible, place multiple easels side by side. Kids are often social and like to talk when they paint. Side-by-side easels also allow you to put one big sheet of paper across all the easels so that kids can collaborate.

Children should be able to draw at several different levels: sitting in a chair at a table, sitting on the floor with a low table or shelf, or on the floor (sitting or lying). The less developed a child's fine-motor skills are, the bigger the paper should be. If a child seems to be stuck in a mode of scribbling, try giving them bigger paper.

As mentioned in chapter 2, motor control starts from the trunk and moves out—essentially gross-motor control happens first and then becomes more controlled and coordinated. If a four-year-old (or an older child) is not yet using a pincer grasp or tripod stance with markers and pencils, encourage more shoulder movements. One way to do this is to put paper under the table and have children lie on their backs to draw. Their arms naturally extend, and they use their upper arms in much the same way as they do for easel painting. You want to start with a child's strength and build off that rather than frustrate them by focusing on skills they have not yet developed.

Drawing through the Ages

You can provide paint or shaving cream to infants because they don't need to be able to grasp to make a mark. They can also make marks with other parts of their bodies: elbows, knees, feet, and so on. It is a sensory experience, but they can also look at the change they are making to the paper.

As older infants and young toddlers gain more control with their hands, you can provide markers or paintbrushes. Both markers and paintbrushes are very forgiving: they don't take a lot of force to make a mark, but they also work if too much force is used. Crayons can also work but are usually too long and thin (even

the chubby crayons). You can also buy crayons that are made to fit in the palm of a child's hand, originally from the company Crayon Rocks (and often referred to generically as crayon rocks), or you can melt crayons in an old muffin tin to make your own. You just need to put the oven on the lowest setting and check on them regularly.

Preschoolers can take on the challenge of drawing with pencils and crayons. You can start with jumbo or chubby pencils and crayons. These can still break if too much force is applied, but they are more forgiving. As children master these, try adding standard pencils and crayons. You can also offer markers of different thicknesses or you can provide short pencils, often called golf pencils, if a child shows the ability to use a pincer grasp but doesn't use it consistently.

It is easier for younger children to draw big since they use their whole arm. Butcher paper

Shawna and Curtis were twins with a sensory processing disorder. They both had a hard time sitting still for long. I never saw Curtis sit still for more than two or three minutes. He often started drawings but rarely finished them. One day I took them to a neighbor's garden. She had flowers on all the borders of her yard. We sat on her lawn in the middle of all these flowers. I gave every child a clipboard and had a few containers of crayons and colored pencils. Curtis lay down on his tummy and drew. Every few minutes he would roll back and forth on the grass. Then he would draw again. All of the kids drew for thirty minutes, including Curtis.

is perfect for several children as well as for one child. You can use it on a table but also on the floor. Have kids sit on the paper or on the edge. When they sit in the middle, they can spin around and around, drawing circles around themselves. The child becomes part of the drawing.

Drawing itself is usually fairly sedentary, not requiring a lot of lower body movement. But children don't need to stay in the room to draw. In fact, there are many things that could inspire drawing outside of the classroom. I have a plastic tote with enough clipboards for my entire class. We have drawn pictures at a neighborhood Laundromat, while outside and looking at street signs, and in a neighbor's garden.

Shawna and Curtis needed to move their whole bodies in order to focus on drawing. Whenever Curtis's attention wandered, he rolled briefly to regain focus. For many children, this ability to move their bodies and then go back to drawing can make this activity more attractive. Standing at a table may also convey the message that full body movement is allowed.

Painting through the Ages

Like drawing, children will start painting with big arm movements and very little finger control, so it makes sense to start with fingerpainting. You can use commercial fingerpaint or any thick tempera paint. You can also use shaving cream (adding a few drops of food coloring if you like), or make fingerpaint by mixing cornstarch and water (you can boil the water for a smoother paint). You can have children paint on trays or cookie sheets. You can also have them paint directly on the table and use a squeegee for cleanup.

You can offer paintbrushes to children as they gain more control with their grasp. It helps to start with thick brushes and gradually move to thinner brushes. You can also use other objects as brushes, such as feathers, willow branches, dandelions, sticks, clay tools, and so forth.

Preschoolers and schoolagers can also pump their own tempera paint. You can buy pumps for gallon jugs of paint. You only need to have red, yellow, blue, and white. Children can mix their own colors. You can make color recipe cards for them to follow. Simply put a dot of each primary color on an index card and then a square or other shape of the resulting color, such as a red dot and a blue dot with a purple square. As they get used to mixing colors, you can add a gallon of black as well. Children will want to pump the paint until they fill the container (see Tom's axioms, page 172), so you don't want to use a paint cup, which holds eight ounces. You can buy small plastic ramekins (two to four ounces) from a restaurant supply store. They are fairly inexpensive (fifty to seventy-five cents), but you usually have to buy forty-eight at a time.

Preschoolers will usually need easel paper, if not bigger (at least twelve by eighteen inches) for painting. They use shoulder movements as well as some wrist movements. As they grow older, they can use more wrist and finger movements. This allows schoolagers to paint on smaller paper. They can still paint big pictures and should still be given opportunities to make big paintings. You can even have older children plan and paint a mural. Children of any age can make a big painting.

Not everyone can create such a big painting, but perhaps you can find ways to go bigger than you have so far. You could try a big painting outdoors. You could

Our center has Painting Day once a year. The culminating activity is a giant painting about twenty-five feet long and fifteen feet across and then six feet up on the wall. We have about thirty kids total, and they take turns painting with brooms, bath sponges, big brushes, and eventually their bodies. We use about three gallons of paint in the hour that it takes. We have lots of teachers on hand to rinse the kids off. The parents are told to dress them in clothes that might not survive. The paint is washable, and most clothes can soak overnight before being washed, but some color might remain. It is exhausting, it is messy, and it is wonderful.

tape together butcher paper or use a smaller sheet of photo backdrop paper. You can buy a big tarp and put the paper on it. It can be on the ground or hanging up. The point is, you want to try to have paper bigger than the child. The kids should feel as if they are inside the painting.

Three-Dimensional Art

Don't forget to include materials for three-dimensional work. Clay is a great material for children (common clay or earthenware is the cheapest and most suitable for the classroom). It takes a lot of force to manipulate clay. Children will often have to stand and alter their stance to form the clay the way they want. Children can push, poke, cut, roll, and twist clay. If the sculpture sits out for a day or two, it will dry enough to be painted. I find that many of my block builders will sculpt with clay because of the tactile nature of the medium.

Keep the clay in a plastic container or plastic bag. You can cover it with a wet cloth if it starts to dry out. You can also make a hole in the middle and add water. The water will absorb into the entire lump of clay. If the clay is very dry or if you have sculptures that are no longer wanted, you can revive the clay. All you have to do is soak it in water and drain it a few hours later. The kids can help with this. If it gets too wet, you can let it sit out for a few hours. I am usually able to use a twenty-five-pound bag of clay for more than a year, occasionally reviving it or recycling sculptures. I spend less than ten dollars on clay a year (much cheaper than paint). Common clay is the clay found in the ground in most places, so you can dig it out of the ground if you want to spend even less.

Recycled materials are great for three-dimensional artwork and a terrific way to reuse something that might otherwise be thrown away. You can have bins for yogurt and applesauce containers and other packaging; old nuts and bolts; craft materials, such as colored feathers and sticks; and scraps of fabric and anything else that you can think of. You can also use larger objects, such as boxes, pieces from broken toys, pieces from old furniture or appliances, and the like. Different materials are going to require different strategies for assembly: glue, tape, string, staples, needle and thread, and such. Children not only will have to problem solve, but will have to use a variety of motor skills for their creations.

Weaving requires a lot of body movement. You can weave ribbon, long grass, rope, or cloth strips. You can use a loom, or a chain-link fence will do. Schoolagers can make a loom with a few pieces of wood and a hammer and nails. The bigger the loom, the more kids can use it and the more body movement involved.

Because some children like to create three-dimensional structures to be used for props, you can stock some materials in the toy area or block area. These could be loose parts or paper and markers. You don't have to stock a lot of art materials in other interest areas, but rather enough to remind them that they can create new props. If they start creating props, they will probably go to the art area if they need more supplies. The point is to spark ideas.

Block Area

Movement is an essential part of block building. In my classroom, the children who move the most are often in the block area. I think this is because children need to go back and forth to add blocks to their structures. At times they have to sit. Other times they have to kneel or stand. With good room arrangement, your block area will probably encourage a lot of movement, as well as great problem-solving skills and experiences with the laws of physics.

Block areas should be located away from high-traffic areas because blocks can fall down easily. On the other hand, block areas need a lot of space, and as I have mentioned, children like to fill empty spaces. If no one is building in the block area, it will be enticing for children as a place to run or roughhouse. This can be a good choice if no one is trying to build. If there are buildings, children generally figure out that they need to refrain from roughhousing or other boisterous play near buildings. Of course, there may be a child who needs help understanding this, and it is a good learning opportunity.

Most young children will need help keeping track of their whole body even if they are trying to be careful. For example, a child may be sitting on the floor working on a block structure. Another building could be behind them, and when they sit down they are very careful not to bump it. As they get involved with their own building, they

may move around to add blocks. Most young children will focus only on their hands at this point and not notice where their feet are. Buildings can get bumped with feet or other parts of the body without intention. Also, many children will have an impulse to push a building down to see and hear the crash, although most will be able to control that impulse. In either case, conflict resolution and reminders of the guideline ("We take care of each other") will come in handy.

Types of Blocks

Preschool classrooms usually have block areas with wooden "unit blocks" making up most of the blocks. Unit blocks are wonderful open-ended toys. The size and shape of the blocks are based on a unit, which is 5.5 inches across and 2.75 inches high (half a unit) and 1.375 inches deep (a quarter of a unit). The other blocks are based on this same unit, only changing in length. Therefore, children can build with blocks in any configuration (vertical, horizontal, or flat), and make stacks of equal height by simply stacking enough blocks or orienting them correctly. This allows children to have a high success rate, which encourages persistence.

Because of the size and weight of the blocks, children have to move back and forth, taking several trips to make a building. They may need to crawl, stretch, and walk to complete a building.

In addition to unit blocks, block areas may have other building blocks as well. Having a variety of blocks allows children to be creative and can encourage problem solving. Toddlers enjoy smaller blocks, sometimes referred to as table blocks, because they fit easier into tiny hands. Just be sure to have plenty of rectangular or square blocks, because toddlers tend to build in one line (straight up or across the floor in a line). Older preschoolers and schoolagers will probably incorporate triangles, arches, and cylinders into their buildings to represent architectural features. These smaller blocks can offer more opportunity for individual creativity than unit blocks, but they offer less opportunity for collaboration and full body movement. They are a great addition to a classroom but are limited in terms of encouraging children to move their bodies.

Some programs may have blocks that are larger than unit blocks, often referred to as hollow blocks because they tend to be hollow. These blocks encourage a lot of body movement. Most children can only carry one block at a time. They also encourage collaboration because of their size. Children can often build structures that a few children can fit on or in. This often leads to pretend play scenarios. Many toddler classrooms have cardboard blocks (usually looking like bricks) that are big, but I find these don't stay flat enough for stacks to stay up. Of course, many toddlers love knocking over the stacks, and cardboard works well to satisfy this impulse. But in terms of building, hollow blocks can be a good choice for toddlers because of their stability. Children can stack two blocks and sit on them and feel a certain pride in the chair they made. Several companies even sell specific sets of hollow blocks with smaller dimensions for toddlers.

The size of hollow blocks can make them difficult to store. I worked in one center where my classroom shared a block area with another classroom in the middle of our two rooms. This allowed us to have a full set of hollow blocks in an otherwise small setting, although the children couldn't save buildings for later use. Some companies are starting to sell outdoor hollow blocks, which can also alleviate some of the concern about space.

Found materials and tree cookies (branches cut crosswise into pieces about one inch thick) can present a building challenge and open up new ideas. The older the children, the better this will work since children need to be successful most of the time. It may be too difficult for toddlers and young preschoolers. Schoolagers may find the challenge just right.

In addition there should be some other items that enhance play with the buildings. You can add cars and other vehicles along with road signs. You can add people or animal figurines. All of these encourage pretend play that may involve more collaboration between children. This, in turn, can motivate children to move around more in various crouched and sitting positions.

Blocks also make good supports for ramps. PVC tubes (cut in half or not), plastic gutters, molding, shelves, planks, or rubber strips can all be used as ramps. Children can send balls, toy cars, and marbles down the ramps.

Big Body Play Area/Boisterous Play Area

A big body play area is not as common in early childhood programs. It is seldom mentioned as a part of classroom environment. Many programs often have a gym, large-muscle room, or outdoor area that allows for big body play, but these are seldom accessible throughout the day. This doesn't allow children to incorporate bigger movements in their dramatic play in the classroom. Usually each class uses the room for a relatively short period of time when compared to the length of time a child spends at the program.

As we learn more about the benefits of big body play and teachers become more comfortable with this type of play, I am hopeful that having a dedicated area in the classroom available for the majority of a child's time in group care will become more common.

A mat can help define this area. In a classroom or family child care, you will

This year I had eight boys and two girls in my class, so I planned on using the mat frequently. What surprised me was that the two girls requested the mat more than anyone. Loretta and Diana liked to play a game I came to call Pile On. Diana would lie down. Loretta would lie on top of her, and so did Fred and Sam. They would all just lie there in a stack until the bottom person would say stop. Then they would all tumble off, giggling. Then it would be someone else's turn. They would do this for twenty or thirty minutes straight, with very little variation. Eventually, the game would evolve into Diana pretending to be the mom. Her babies would each lie on one of the colored rectangles on the mat. It wasn't the roughest play, but it was always full body play.

probably need to have children roughhouse on their knees. In a family child care program, you may want a separate mat for toddlers. Toddlers haven't developed the sense of their own strength and how to handicap (for smaller children). Many family care providers have told me that toddlers often want to join in roughhousing but get hurt because they don't read the body language of others very well. What I have found works best is to have a separate mat for toddlers and have big cushions or pillows for them to wrestle. The teacher makes a good wrestling partner too because they are better able to handle it when a toddler gets too rough.

This area should be free of toys so children can play with abandon while still taking care of one another. There could be pillows and cushions to crash into or throw. If there is more room, you could have exercise balls or exercise peanuts for children to bounce on.

In my own classroom, we do not have enough room for a separate big body play area. Instead, we have mats we can take out when needed. I have a very small classroom (625 square feet), so we often have to be creative. We usually put the mats in the block area. This generally works because the kids who use the mats the most are also the ones who build with blocks the most. When the block area has buildings in it, we usually move the table from the dramatic play area and put the mats there. We have also moved the table out of the art area. We simply view the placement of the mats as a problem to be solved, and we always figure it out.

Book Area/Library

No matter what the area is called—book area, bookshelf, or library—it is a place to find books. You may also have books in other interest areas. For example, if the children often build spaceships in the toy area, you may have books about outer space or aliens on the shelves. Most of the books will be in the book area, but the books are the starting point. Just as the stories don't need to stay inside the book, the enjoyment of books doesn't need to stay inside the book area.

You should read to children one-on-one and in small groups, as well as with the whole group. You should also encourage children to act out the stories. You may have costumes and props or flannel boards that will encourage this. You may have group times where you act out a story with them.

You should also tell stories to children. Storytelling is different than reading books in several ways. Because the storyteller and listeners interact, you can change the story whenever you want. You can incorporate the names of the children listening. You can also have the children add to the story. You may ask the younger children simply to suggest one detail at a time. As they get older, children may add to the story line itself. Schoolagers can make up their own stories and even create books based on them.

Storytelling allows for more movement than books. While you can have children do movements for parts of a book, you usually can't join them because you are holding the book. Also, the children can't focus on their movement as easily because they are trying to look at the book. With storytelling, children can watch you do the movement and join in. You don't even have to tell them how to move. They will pick it up by watching.

How to Tell Stories

The art of storytelling has been part of the human experience for millennia. There are master storytellers who take years to hone their skills, but you do not need to be a master to get started. Everyone tells stories at some point, even if the stories are just about events in their own lives. Here are some basics points that can get you started.

If you are new to storytelling, you can start with a fairy tale. You can simply retell the story as you remember it, or you can change the names or the settings to reflect your audience. One I have been telling for several years is *The Meanest Teacher*, which is essentially *The Emperor's New Clothes* set in a child care center. The kids can't get enough of the teacher being outsmarted.

As you get comfortable, you can create your own stories. I make up three or four stories a week. Most of them are soon forgotten, but there are a few that children request over and over. One strategy that seems to connect with children is to choose a trait that many of the children exhibit and make that a starting point for a character. One time a parent told me that she was concerned that her child kept mixing up the terms *front* and *back*, as well as *up* and *down*. The story that day was about a new character named Backward Bob. Bob was a grown-up who always did things backward. Someone would have to tell him, "That's backward, Bob." The story would end with him saying, "Yep. Backward Bob, that's my name."

You can learn a few tricks from picture books as well. It's a good idea to have a refrain, a set of words that repeats throughout the story. Children quickly learn to repeat this along with you. This is a great time to add a simple movement so that every time the words repeat, so does the action. Adding a few sound effects also draws in the listeners. If a cat walks into the room, what sound does it make? *Slink slink? Pitter pat? Clickity click? Meoooow?* Children will join in for these as well. That's one of the great things about making up stories for young children: you get immediate feedback. If something gets a laugh, you can repeat the joke as a refrain. If a child says some of the words or sound effects with you, repeat that.

As you start telling stories, you may find that you get stuck. Don't panic! You can simply ask, "What do you think happened next?" You will get several answers, and you can choose one (or all) of them. "As a matter of fact, aliens did show up . . ."

Nonfiction Books

Book areas should also have nonfiction books. Nonfiction books can seem dry and the last thing that will keep a child's interest, but they can actually spur a lot of interest and a lot of movement. The topics have to relate to children's current interests or to their experiences. It is also important to remember that nonfiction books are read differently than fiction books. You can skip around the books for the information you need.

Most of the nonfiction books in your classroom should be about familiar things. These familiar or day-to-day topics can lead to explorations or investigations. The books may be about trees or flowers. They could be about grocery stores or firefighters. Sometimes fiction books can also lead to investigations.

One spring I read the picture books *Knuffle Bunny* and *A Pocket for Corduroy*, both of which take place in Laundromats. The kids started talking about Laundromats. It turned out that none of them had been to a Laundromat. I took them to visit a Laundromat that was a few blocks from our school. After that we spent the next eight weeks investigating Laundromats.

We visited the Laundromat a few times a week. We watched a video on how to do laundry (made for college students) and then brought a load of laundry to the Laundromat. We also tried washing clothes in two buckets, one where we agitated the laundry with a stick and one where we let it sit in the bucket. We tried drying laundry three ways: some on a clothesline, some in a clothes dryer, and some left in a pile. We had a repair person show us how he runs a washer cycle with the lid open to test it. This all started from a couple of picture books and a conversation.

Dramatic Play/Dress-Up/Pretend Play Area

During dramatic play or pretending, children often immerse themselves in play and lose track of time. Anyone who has asked children to clean up when they are in the middle of a pretend play scenario knows this. I could have children play for over an hour, and if they are playing family, they will complain that they haven't had time to play. This play encourages a lot of social interactions, rich conversations, and movement. Almost all scenarios will involve motion. If children are pretending to sleep, one of them will announce that it is morning. I find a lot of pretend play eventually leads to chase: a baby crawls away, a bad guy gets away, a fire needs to be put out, and so on.

Pretend play changes as children grow. Older infants begin to imitate those around them. Toddlers often imitate animals and vehicles. Preschoolers will start to become more creative with pretending, creating scenarios that get more complex and involve more children. Preschoolers can become immersed in their roles, insisting that they really are Batman (or some other role). Schoolagers continue pretending, sometimes turning the play into physical games (such as chase). Other children may have a continuous story line that pauses until they resume the story the next day.

Toddlers usually engage in play based on real objects or situations. They need a few simple props to support their pretend play. Usually some animal costumes as well as props that mirror their home life, such as dishes and pots and pans, will suffice. If the adults in their lives wear certain uniforms or use certain tools, you might want to provide some version of those items. Toddlers usually need objects that are pretty similar to the object they are representing.

Preschoolers start adding to their repertoire. They continue to play animals or some aspect of family life, but they also start imitating others in the community, such as doctors, firefighters, construction workers, etc. They will also pretend to be magical characters, roles that they don't encounter in their daily lives. This can include princesses, knights, pirates, queens, fairies, superheroes, aliens, pirates, monsters, and bad guys. During the preschool years, children may blend fantasy roles and day-to-day roles or talk about pretend scenarios in the same way they talk about real life.

This is not to say that children don't know the difference between fantasy and reality; they just don't see anything wrong with blurring the line between the two. This year in my class, four-year-old Greg often planned to "take over the school" with a few other children. They would spend hours talking about the plans and drawing maps. I saw this as a way for them to feel more powerful in the benevolent dictatorship that is a classroom. A few months later, Greg confided in me that he wasn't really going to take over the school; it was just a game. I told him I felt a lot better knowing that, but then I asked what we could do to make sure no one else takes over the school. Without missing a beat, he told me that he was a ninja, and he would protect the school. Greg easily slipped from fantasy to reality and back again. All the while, he still followed the classroom routine and guidelines. He always acted as if it was a game, but he only admitted it the one time.

During the preschool years, children are able to use props or costumes that have some attribute of the object they represent, but they don't need it to resemble that object. For example, a rectangular block might be a phone (for those who have been teaching as long as I have, you may remember when the arch block represented a phone). This is also the time when anything shaped like the letter L will be used as a pretend gun. This can drive adults crazy, but it is an indication of how well children are able to imagine the details (for more on warplay see pages 96–102).

Schoolagers still engage in pretend play, but as they get older, they need fewer props. There should still be toys and natural materials (sticks, pinecones, etc.), but specific props are less necessary. What they need more than anything is time and space where they are not interrupted.

There are a few things you can do to encourage more body movement with pretend play. One is to locate the dramatic play area near the block area or toy area to allow crossover play. Children can make props that can be used in any of the areas. Preschoolers and younger schoolagers will probably benefit from this the most, although toddlers and other schoolagers may as well.

Children should also have a variety of spaces to pretend in. The dramatic play area may be the place to find costumes or specific furniture (toy stoves, sinks, etc.), but different scenarios will require different types of places. If children pretend to ride on a bus or train, they need a space to line up chairs. If they need

How I Learned to Stop Worrying and Love the Couch

I pushed the new couch into the nook with a feeling of satisfaction. It was supposed to fit with an inch to spare, but after spending a few hundred dollars, I didn't relax until it was put in. It was just the right size for an odd indentation in my dramatic play area (courtesy of some concealed ductwork). I had a carpet that fit the rectangle of the space, leaving a two-foot bald spot on one side. I was more than thrilled to find this couch that not only provided a cozy play space but would also cover up the floor.

The first few weeks, the kids used the couch as a crib, a car, a couch, and a hospital bed. I had found a perfect solution to my problem. But then something happened. One of the kids figured out that if you pulled the couch out from the wall, it created the perfect hideout. The hideout also became a tree house, a tent, and a bedroom. Every day it was something new. And every day, as the couch was pushed forward, the rug would scrunch up until it was getting ruined. And if that wasn't enough, the arm of the couch was chipping the paint a bit.

I tried to stop the kids from pulling the couch out. That didn't work, of course. I tried to be there when they moved the couch, but every time I walked over, the couch was moved, and the rug was bunched up.

I tried to show them how to lift it on top of the rug. That wasn't any more successful. I was getting quite frustrated. I could only flatten the rug back so many times before it was ruined. I could stay late and paint the wall, but how long would that last?

When I finally stepped back, I saw a different picture. The kids were showing me they wanted a small space to play in. They also seemed to take satisfaction in being the creators of this space. The stumbling block was the carpet, which was made up of smaller square tiles. I decided to remove one more row to see what would happen. It left a bigger bald spot, which bothered me, but I've lived with bald spots before.

The next day the kids pulled the couch out until it touched the rug. A father who worked as a contractor asked if I needed anything done, and I showed him the chipped paint. He brought in a few scraps of wainscoting and covered the walls. Suddenly, the area looked inviting again. And the kids continued to use the space behind the couch. It doesn't matter how many years I have been doing this, I still find myself taking on battles that I can't win. When I focus on the needs of the kids, I can usually find a way where we both win.

to go to bed, they need a small, cozy space. Children love to go in small spaces. In pretend play, it often means a tent, a hideout, a crib, or a jail. When designing a classroom, there should be small spaces that fit only two or three children.

Some pretend play may get a bit boisterous. Cushions or pillows give children a space to crash into. Children can learn to use these soft areas (or how to create their own) so they can stay safe while playing boisterously. This encourages the big body play they need, and it is easier for the teacher to occasionally guide a child to a safe spot than to prohibit this type of play. Of course, if you have a big body play area, they can move to that area as well.

Be sure to provide props that encourage different types of pretending. Capes, toy tools, and steering wheels may lead to louder, more active play. Dishes, a stove, and play food may lead to children sitting at a table. Both types of play are important. As you observe your class playing, you can make changes to follow their interests.

Gym/Gross-Motor Room

Many programs have a room devoted to big body play. There are usually balls, climbing structures, and often bikes. All of these are great, but remember that some children, especially girls, are more likely to play physically if the teachers do (Carlson 2011a). You should plan on playing physically for at least some of the time. When choosing equipment, think about what skills you want children to experience. There should be equipment to climb on and jump from, and places to run, roughhouse, and roll. There should be balls or other objects to throw, kick, and catch. There should also be materials to lift and carry. Mats will be needed wherever there is a fall zone or roughhousing. All these objects can be purchased, but some things can be made or found. A climbing structure, balance beams, or balance boards can be made. Loose parts, such as tires or planks, can be used as well.

Music Area

Playing music is essentially coordinated movements with an instrument. Of course children will turn just about anything into a percussion instrument, but it is a good idea to have other instruments available. It is easier to find percussion instruments that can stand up to the love and attention of a classroom of children, but you can find some tonal instruments. Handbells, small xylophones, and Boomwhackers are some examples. Preschoolers start to discern different tones at this age, so it is good to have instruments they can experiment with. Schoolagers may benefit from a songbook that they help make. It can simply be the lyrics to a few familiar songs with pictures for the nonreaders.

I also like to have a music player that children can operate. We still use a CD player in my room because the buttons can withstand the constant button pushing as children flip between songs to find the one they want. Any player will do, but children should have access to a variety of styles of music from a variety of cultures.

The music area is also often a dance area, so there should be room to move. You can encourage movement with materials that exaggerate movement, such as dancing ribbons and scarves. You can also have costumes associated with the music. I often have rock-star bracelets, gloves, and wigs, as well as toy microphones and fake guitars that I made out of cardboard, duct tape, and broom handles. The items you have to get kids moving will depend on the children. I added the toy guitars after watching a child pretend he was playing guitar on a toy broom every day (eventually knocking off the bristles). I also find that mirrors encourage children to dance.

Neighborhood/Expanded School Yard

Neighborhoods usually aren't considered an interest area, which is a shame. The recent interest in social studies for preschoolers will hopefully return interest in the neighborhood. There is so much learning that can happen in the neighborhood. Children learn about other people who live nearby, various jobs that make up the community, and the plants and animals that live around the program while also keeping their bodies moving.

Exploration of a neighborhood allows children hands-on experience to learn about their environment and community roles. The walking that happens makes the children more attentive and gives them more opportunities to move.

Obviously the type of learning will depend on the setting. If there are houses surrounding the program, children can see the variety of homes and yards. Hopefully they can get to know a few of the neighbors by name. You could help the kids make food to bring to neighbors to initiate the relationship. Perhaps there is an elder who is unable to leave the house and would welcome visitors. Churches or community centers may be able to help you make those connections.

If you have businesses in the area, you can take field trips to learn more about the business or invite the owner or workers to your program to talk about what they do. You could take the children to a store to shop for something for your classroom. Perhaps there is a nursing home or assisted living facility where you could arrange regular visits or arrange a pen pal program, where each child makes drawings or letters for individual residents.

If you are in a rural environment, you can have the children adopt a tree that they can visit throughout the year. They can learn the name of the tree and watch it change through the seasons. Perhaps children will collect things from the tree or draw pictures of the tree.

Walks

On any walk, remember that the emphasis should be on the journey, not the destination, in the same way that we focus on the process, not the product, with art activities. Too often teachers take children on walks outdoors to get to a certain place. Every effort is made to make that walk efficient. Children are often made to walk in a straight line or hold a rope. This can keep the children from stopping to look at things along the way, but that is exactly the problem. We should be encouraging children's curiosity, not stifling it.

My center is in an urban neighborhood. The neighborhood is mostly made up of single-family homes with front yards and backyards. We are two blocks from the Mississippi River. Since its inception over forty years ago as a parent cooperative, the center has been part of the neighborhood. One of the first teachers put it this way: "The neighborhood was the curriculum." That is still true today (or at least it is *part* of the curriculum).

We have our own playground, but we venture out regularly. On our walks, we often have to stop when children find ants on the sidewalk. The same is true for flowers or leaves or walnuts. I also always have a garbage bag so we can pick up trash along the way. It is part of our third classroom guideline, "We help our community."

There is a parkway we call The Giving Tree named after a giant willow tree. The area is wide enough to play on (more than fifty feet) without being too close to the nearby roads. There

are dozens of trees, which also means an endless supply of sticks, acorns, walnuts, and so on. On our block, there is a neighbor with a small pond. We check on the pond throughout the year to watch the progress of the water plants, the fish, and (later) the ice. We have a park we walk to that takes us under a highway overpass, which also has sloped concrete that presents a small challenge to children who try to walk on the incline to the park. We also visit a grocery store. Most important, however, is our neighbor Barbara, who has gardens lining the sidewalks on her corner lot. The gardens are full of flowers but also lots of ornaments and objects. She has a whole section of gears from some ancient machine and another section with figurines of animals.

The children love passing Barbara's garden. In fact, we can often spend five, ten, even fifteen minutes just walking by her house. One time, four-year-old Dale came up with the idea to take pictures of some of the objects in the gardens. The next day we brought the pictures with us and kids had to find the objects. A few months later, Barbara was notified by the city to "clean up" her yard. She appealed. The children brought her the photos. I had written their comments about the garden on the photos as well. Barbara used the photos (along with testimony from many neighbors) to win her appeal, and her garden is still a magical place of discovery.

In fact, anywhere we walk can be a magical place of discovery if we just take the time to look.

Outdoor Area/Playground

There are a wide variety of outdoor areas in the early childhood field. Some programs share a playground with others and have little control over what structures or materials are available. Some programs have an outdoor space that consists only of human-made ground surfaces and commercial climbing structures. Some have acres of space, and some have a few hundred square feet. You may or may not be able to use all the information provided in this section. I suggest that you observe how the children in your care use the space and see if they are moving their bodies. See if they are finding physical challenges that keep them engaged for extended periods of time.

Children need a sensory diet with a variety of experiences. There is no place better than outdoors. The environment changes with the weather. There are usually a variety of surfaces to walk or sit on, and a variety of materials to manipulate, including natural materials, which don't have the uniformity that purchased toys have. Children can be louder outdoors without interrupting children who don't like loud noises. There is more room for vigorous play without bumping into others.

Because being outdoors is so important, it is good to plan for all kinds of weather. Children should go out every day unless there is hazardous weather, such as lightning or severe storms. Children can play in rain and snow, heat or cold—they just need to dress for it. You can ask parents to bring appropriate clothing, but it is also a good idea to have some extra outdoor clothing on hand. You may also need to make sure children drink water on hot days. You should be aware of any heat or cold advisories and adjust the duration of your time outside, but it is still important to have children experience all kinds of weather.

There should also be things to climb on. While some of that may be commercial climbing equipment, it should not be the only thing available to climb. Commercial playground equipment has become so focused on "safety" that most of it offers very little challenge for children. Children aren't able to engage in a wide variety of movement experiences. There are usually stairs and slides and perhaps ladders. Most children figure out that climbing up the slide presents a good challenge.

Teachers sometimes worry about children climbing up slides, but it is not inherently dangerous. The height of the potential fall is the same going up or down, so if the slide is safe to go down, it is safe to go up. If you have a small group of children, you can have them check before going up or down to see if anyone is in the way. If you have a bigger group, you can make up and down signs and alternate which way to go on the slide, such as in the morning you go up, in the afternoon you go down.

Natural materials can also be used for climbing. Logs, stumps, trees, straw bales, and hills can all present physical challenges for kids to keep the play exciting while helping with their physical development.

We have a small playground (1,800 square feet) at our urban center. We have a small commercial climbing structure made of cedar. We also have a hill about four feet high. The hill was originally covered in grass, but the shade from the surrounding houses and trees as well as the extreme amount of foot traffic killed all the grass. The hill started to erode, so we covered it in outdoor carpet. At first we worried that the carpet would stand out from all the natural materials (the rest of the yard is covered in woodchips). However, the carpet soon had enough dirt tracked on it that it looked like the rest of the yard after a few weeks.

As we started incorporating more natural materials (tree stumps, tree cookies, branches, etc.), we found that the climber took up too much space. Since it was made out of wood, we were able to take out half of it. After we removed it, children had more room to build with our outdoor blocks. Other children used the extra space to jump off the climber. Still others used the space for more chasing. Children were moving around more, and the play was more vigorous.

One of the girls, Loretta, asked me to play chase every day when we were outside. The first two weeks she didn't actually play chase, but she watched the others run away as I chased after them. Eventually she joined in. My favorite memory of Loretta was at a park where other children were attacking trees with sticks, pretending they were monsters. She looked at me, stick in hand, and said, "There's a monster." The two of us ran at the tree and struck it with our swords until we defeated the monster. We didn't celebrate long, however, before Loretta pointed to another tree, "Another monster!" We were off.

Outdoors is a great place to roughhouse. There is more space, so kids have an easier time finding a place where they won't interrupt others and where they have less chance of bumping into hard objects. They will probably be able to roughhouse standing up outside. Depending on the size of your outdoor space, you may need to designate an area for roughhousing. However, if possible, I think it is better to have the children find a space each day depending on where others are playing. You can help guide them as they self-assess the risks (both of injury and the interruption of others). This way they can make roughhousing part of whatever game they are playing. (For specifics on roughhousing, see pages 93–96.)

Outdoor Classrooms

There has been a trend of referring to the outdoor space as an *outdoor classroom*. I use the term guardedly. If the classroom has a big body play area and allows children to use their whole bodies and there is a commitment to children actively learning, then the term *classroom* seems fine. My fear is that using the term will encourage teachers to focus on sit-down activities or perhaps create enclosed interest areas. Just like inside, interest areas should serve as an organizing system to let children know where to find materials and where to put them back. They should not limit what a child can do or where materials can be used.

Outdoor areas can allow children to do many of the same things they do inside but in different ways. For example, I have seen kids playing music that would have been disruptive indoors, or kids getting messy while creating things with loose parts outdoors. Kids can immerse their whole bodies in a sandbox, which is essentially a large sensory table. The concept of an outdoor classroom can be a good way to design the space, but you should expect and encourage kids to move more when they are outside.

Gardening

If your program is open in the summer or is in a warmer climate, I strongly encourage gardening with the children. The garden can be as small as one window box or a larger flowerpot, or even an old car tire. The garden can certainly be bigger if you have the space without taking away from room to run and play. When they garden, children learn to care for living things while learning where their food comes from. They also have to use their bodies in ways that they might not when playing. And like other real work, they feel a sense of pride in the work and a sense of belonging to a community.

Gardening involves planting, watering, weeding, and harvesting. Most young children may only work on the garden for a few minutes, but they will probably play in the dirt while you and a few others work on the garden, so leave space unplanted. Most children like to play in water, so allow for water play while you water the garden if you can. Every few days, be sure to point out the garden. Show them what to look for: the white flowers turning into green berries and finally the bright red strawberries.

I find that children are more likely to eat vegetables they have grown. One time my class ate an entire broccoli plant. First I cut off the florets and dunked them in water. After we ate all those, I cut off the stems, which were soon devoured. Within ten minutes, only the wide base was left.

Water

I mentioned water for indoor messy play, but there is a lot more potential for using water outdoors. Children can make it move with just a simple garden hose or a hand pump. Moving water encourages a lot of sustained body movement. Children often try to follow the water as it travels. If there isn't the potential to keep water continuously flowing, you can use elevation. You can use plastic gutters, PVC tubing, troughs, or plastic bottles anchored in some way. Children can pour the water at the top and watch it flow down. Of course the kids don't just watch it go down. They follow it with their bodies. They block the flow whenever possible. They try to catch the water in cups, shovels, spoons, or even their hands.

Fire

Fire is an element that is not often used in programs for young children in the United States, but it presents a lot of fascination and excitement for children. Constant adult supervision is needed, and adults should take care to make sure the fire is put out safely. As long as you don't have the fire in an area where children are usually running, it is fairly easy to keep it safe. Children can feel the heat before they actually get burned. If you build the fire in a metal ring or bowl, you will have to make sure children know not to touch it. Otherwise, I find that I don't have to remind children to be careful. They can self-assess the risk fairly well. The Norwegian researcher Ellen Beate Hansen Sandseter (2013) lists fire as one of the types of risk that children seek. Fire can be fascinating to watch. You can make snack on the fire with long sticks or with a grill. You can cook fruit, such as pineapples, peaches, and apples, as well as meat and, of course, marshmallows.

Loose Parts: Natural Materials

It's good to have materials that children can use and manipulate. Straw bales, mud, sticks, and pinecones are all examples of loose parts. Straw bales are a great material because kids can build with them, climb on them, or just move them around. It often takes more than one child to move them, so the kids are exercising both their muscles and their social skills. Straw bales do have to be replaced at least annually, but they are still far cheaper than commercial playground equipment and offer so much more for children to do. The fact that they have to be replaced also allows you to reevaluate how many you want and what you will do with them—something you can't easily do with commercial climbing structures.

Dirt is a material that will change with the weather. Children can dig holes. They can use pots and pans or plates and bowls to pretend. Sometimes the dirt will be very dry, and other times it will be gooey mud. Like other sensory materials, there are limitless possibilities in terms of what the children could do.

Trees give us many loose parts: sticks, logs, bark, stumps, and tree cookies. Tree cookies are cross sections of tree limbs or trunk. They can be small, just an inch or two in diameter, or they can be large, two feet or more. You can usually ask a tree service or a parent with a chain saw to make some for you from limbs that would normally end up as wood chips. Most tree parts are bigger and heavier than other loose parts. This encourages a lot of movement because children can move only one or two pieces at a time.

Natural Loose Parts

- stones
- stumps
- sand
- gravel

- twigs
- logs
- tree cookies
- shells

- seedpods
- pinecones
- straw bales

Loose Parts: Human-Made Materials

Loose parts can also be human-made. Children can use cardboard boxes, crates, milk jugs, and fabric, or outdoor blocks or other toys. You can even bring some toys from the classroom outside. Some materials might need to be stored inside or in a shed to protect them from the elements, but that shouldn't stop you from using them.

Some loose parts might be things that children can climb on, such as wooden planks, crates, or tires. Other loose parts can be used to build structures to play in, such as crates and fabric, as well as planks and tires. Other loose parts can be used for creating props for play or simply works of art. The idea is to have open-ended items that children can use in a variety of ways to engage a variety of motor skills.

Human-Made Loose Parts

- large fabric (ripstop nylon, bedsheets, etc.)
- milk jugs (you can fill with water or sand for weight)
- crates
- rope
- tires
- boxes
- pallets
- balls
- buckets
- baskets
- crates

Science Area

Science learning happens throughout the day and in many ways. Children interact with nature when they are outside. They might also help take care of plants or pets in the classroom. They learn about their own bodies when they eat, use

the bathroom, and move their whole bodies. They learn the principles of physics when they crash things, drop things, throw things, or crash their bodies or fall. The science area usually refers to a specific shelf or table that has natural artifacts, such as pinecones, eggshells, or a scientific tool, such as a balance (scale) or a microscope.

Most scientific learning will *not* take place in a science area. This is probably more the case for science than any other interest area. Nevertheless, having a shelf, baskets, or another designated place for science tools or artifacts that otherwise might not be present inside in the classroom or easily accessible outside is necessary.

The best way to teach science to preschoolers is to inspire them to wonder. Let them be researchers. Let them come up with questions. Let them explore. They will come up with several hypotheses to answer their questions. They will test those hypotheses, and they and their "colleagues" will narrow down the possibilities.

Science is mostly about the things we see every day but don't notice. Most of us probably couldn't explain why the sky is blue or what part of the branch leaves grow on and what parts they don't. And it's okay that we don't have the answers. What we need to do is help children ask those questions about the everyday things and then help them figure out how to answer their questions. Science is about wonder.

Breaking Out of the Box

A teacher (or other adult) can help foster this sense of wonder by offering time and tools. Children need to be in nature for long, unstructured periods of time where they naturally make discoveries. Piquing their interest often starts with collecting small objects: stones, nuts, leaves, or dandelions. As children collect, they notice similarities and differences.

An adult (or older child) can help the child reflect on what they have discovered. The adult can ask open-ended questions, taking the time to hear the child's answers rather than provide answers. "Tell me about these." "How could I find some?" The adult can also introduce "wonder" questions. "I wonder if . . ." "I wonder what would happen if you . . ."

If children are going to be scientists, they also need tools. Tools can help children see things they can't otherwise see. Magnifying glasses are often provided, but I have found that they don't provide much that a child can't see by looking closer. On the other hand, a portable stereomicroscope is fairly inexpensive and can be brought outside. Unlike compound microscopes, which require specimens to be mounted on slides, stereomicroscopes allow the specimen to be simply placed under the lens. Worms and insects can crawl under the lens. Pinecones, leaves, or any object less than four inches in width can fit, and the lenses can be focused on different parts of the object. Children can often see patterns on wings and leaves invisible to the naked eye. For younger children who may have a hard time looking into the microscope, you can hold a camera to one of the eyepieces, and children can look at the camera's screen.

In my preschool classroom, one girl watched a worm move across the base of the microscope. She noticed that the setae on the worm helped it move across the base of the microscope. After watching it, she held the worm and felt it tickle her hand. She realized she was feeling the setae. She had felt this before, but looking in the microscope helped her notice it.

Another way for children to "see what they can't see" is to open up the object. Hammers, knives, and saws can be used by children over the age of three with adult supervision. Hammers can be used to crack nuts and other hard objects. Pumpkin carving knives can be used to open many firm vegetables. Depending on the size of the group and the abilities of the children, other knives could be used as well. An adult should hold the object unless it is big enough to stay still on its own. Saws can be used to open many other things, such as markers, balls, and so on (see page 180 for more on using saws).

Many appliances or machines can be opened with screwdrivers. You or another adult should open it first to remove any power source (i.e., cut cords and remove batteries), transformers, and resistors. Children are often fascinated by looking inside these machines. While children can't open up every appliance on a whim, they may look closer at machines that they otherwise might have looked right past.

Giving children time and tools to explore the world around them allows them to be scientists researching the world around them. They are not just opening a walnut or a seedpod or a washing machine. They are opening a door to a new world. They are opening themselves up to wonder.

Sensory Station or Table

As mentioned in chapter 2, children can use tactile experiences to self-regulate. Sensory tables are often the place for children to get these experiences. They can be filled with water, sand, grains, beans, or wood shavings. Some children seem to gravitate to this type of play. I used to try to change the material frequently to give the sensory table some novelty. It seemed as though either no one used the sensory table or there were seven or eight kids all trying to find room around the table. Whenever one child moved the sand in front of them, it would push some sand into another child's self-proclaimed territory. Before I knew it, I was trying to help resolve a conflict over which grains of sand belong to which child.

Then I met Tom Bedard, a preschool teacher with more than thirty years of experience. Tom loves children, but he also loves cardboard almost as much. Tom uses a sensory table as a support for the apparatuses that he creates out of cardboard. Rather than just a table, it becomes a sensory station. This opened a new world to me.

Whether you use cardboard isn't important. What is important is that you forget about the table and think about the sensory experiences of the child. Sensory tables are considered important for young children because they allow children to fill and empty containers and experiment with volume and gravity. The table is simply a way to contain the mess (a bit). What Tom adds to the equation is the idea of having multiple levels, multiple spaces, and multiple holes. Often this means the play goes beyond the table into other containers (buckets, boxes, or another sensory table). It also means that not only can the "table" fit more children without them getting in one another's way, but it also encourages kids to collaborate. One child may send sand down a ramp to another child at the other end. Meanwhile, other children may be at a different level playing factory.

The collaborative nature of this type of multilevel, multiple-space sensory station also allows children who have high arousal or are sensitive about personal space to find a way to play where they have a defined space but can still interact with others.

Children are often bending, kneeling, squatting, and stretching because of the various spaces and levels. A child in a wheelchair may be able to access a level while another child may be standing at a higher level or sitting on the floor at a lower level. At a typical sensory table, children often stand in one place and move only their hands. This is a way to engage the whole child, body and mind.

Axioms of Sensorimotor Play by Tom Bedard (2015)

Axiom	Corollary
1. Children need to transport whatever is in the table out of the table.	During the transporting, children will spill.
2. Children will explore all spaces in any given apparatus no matter how big or small.	More spaces equal more exploration.
3. Children will find all the different levels of play for any given apparatus.	Children will use all levels of play, including the highest and the lowest, which includes the floor.
4. Children are naturally drawn to pouring, rolling, or sliding materials and objects down ramps, chutes, and tubes.	
5. Children are compelled by nature to put things in holes.	Children will find every hole in and around an apparatus no matter how big or small. Children, whenever possible, will modify the holes of any given apparatus.
6. Children will try to stop or redirect the flow of any medium in the table for any given apparatus.	Children, whenever possible, will try to completely block the flow of any medium.
7. Children will always devise new and novel activities and explorations with the materials presented that are tangential to the apparatus itself.	
8. Children will fill any and all containers with the medium or materials provided.	Children need to empty any and all filled containers.

Toy/Manipulative Area

A toy area should encourage curiosity, creativity, and movement. Most toys should be open-ended, allowing children to use the toys in several ways. Loose parts work very well for this and should be used along with commercial toys. The toy area should be located in such a way that children can play alone or collaborate.

The toy area is essentially the place for tummy time for infants. As mentioned earlier, they need time to play on their tummies to build up muscles and develop muscle control. There should be carpeting and only a few toys out at a time. If you have preschoolers or schoolagers in the same group, you need a way to physically separate small toys that could pose a choking hazard. Storing toys for infants in bins or baskets on a high shelf can be helpful. You can bring out new toys as needed, but be sure to leave space on the floor for the infants who can cruise around.

Toddlers can have more toys on low shelves that are accessible to them throughout freeplay. Find a balance between enough choices to make play interesting but not so many that making choices becomes difficult. Remember, one of the main ways children play at this age is dumping out bins of toys. This is an important experience that helps them learn about cause and effect, gravity, and momentum, and it is an awful lot of fun. If the children are really engaged with the toys, it is quite possible that all the toys will be dumped out. Make sure cleanup is manageable for the children (with your help of course). You may want to put some additional toys on high shelves to bring down as needed to help balance the toddlers' need for organization to feel in control and their need for creating chaos.

Preschoolers can have more toys on low shelves and should be able to move them from place to place. Shelves should be near open floor space for children to spread out when they are using toys. Children should be allowed to bring toy bins to other places if they would rather sit at a table or use the toys as part of a pretend play scenario in the dramatic play area. Children should also be free to bring the toys to a table or to the floor so they can choose how to anchor themselves (sitting, kneeling, standing, etc.). Children are more likely to be creative with the toys if they can move about freely.

Schoolagers can handle more choices and can reach more shelves. They also may play more games with rules, as well as play with toys with smaller and smaller parts. Schoolagers will probably use toys at tables more often, but they should have the choice of sitting elsewhere like preschoolers. They can also benefit from having a mix of toys and loose parts.

Loose Parts for Inside (Note: children under the age of three should not have loose parts that could be choking hazards.)

- shower curtain rings
- measuring cups
- milk jugs (you can fill with water or sand for weight)
- stones
- twigs
- shells
- seedpods
- pinecones
- boxes
- baskets

Writing Area

While writing is an activity that is done with little movement, there are still some changes you can implement to make your classroom more body friendly. For preschoolers and even some young schoolagers, sitting in a chair may not yet be an automatic process. It is easier for these children to focus on the motor skills necessary for writing if their bodies are anchored. For some children, this will mean lying down on the floor with their shoulders raised. Others will want to sit on the floor with a low writing surface. Others may want to write at a table, but they may put one knee on a chair rather than sitting down. Obviously, a table with a few chairs and writing implements isn't enough.

Have clipboards available so that children can move to where they are comfortable writing. Having several different types of paper to meet various needs, such as lined paper, index cards, and paper strips, is helpful. This allows even young preschoolers to make a sign for a block building without having to cut paper to the correct size. They are much more likely to write something if they don't have other steps to carry out first. Having reference materials, such as a sheet with the alphabet, cards with words to copy, or wordbooks (books with pictures and the word underneath), can be helpful. The reference material should be in the native languages of the children in the class. These materials should be portable so that kids don't have to stay at a table to use them.

Also keep in mind that the development of writing skills depends on many physical skills. Children need to have a lot of experience moving their whole bodies—climbing, rocking, and so forth. Infants and toddlers are working on skills that lead to writing when they chew on toys, dump out toys, crawl, run, and knock things down. Preschoolers will start using their hands to make marks with increasing precision. Even with preschoolers, most of this will happen in

the art area rather than a writing area. As they develop the motor coordination and the understanding of the purpose of writing and the alphabetic principle, preschoolers will benefit from the materials in a writing area.

Schoolagers will use writing much more often. You can encourage writing by including it in other activities, such as writing stories to act out, writing notes for the next day, and so on. The reference materials will change. Dictionaries and computers for reference can come in handy. For motor development, it is still important for children to learn how to write by hand and not just rely on keyboarding. Remember that writing is simply a very coordinated motor skill, but it relies on large-motor skills for anchoring the body as well as fine-motor skills. The writing area should meet all of these motor needs.

Workbench/Tools

As mentioned in chapter 2, heavy work helps children self-regulate. Using real woodworking tools is a great way for children to do heavy work. They can also see the effect of their efforts, whether they are building or taking things apart. Some preschool and school-age classrooms have workbenches with tools, but many teachers still avoid this type of activity. This might be because some teachers do not have much experience with tools themselves. However, children need

experience with tools so they have a foundation for creativity and inquiry to build on. This is a simple extension of the tools that are more common in preschool, such as scissors, paintbrushes, and magnifying glasses. Successful experiences with tools allow children to problem solve better in the future because they have more options to explore. If you are inexperienced with a particular tool, try it out yourself as part of your preparation for using tools.

Fear of injury may also make teachers hesitant to use real tools. However, the presence of a workbench actually allows children to learn how to use tools safely. Teachers can establish a few ground rules to help children be successful and safe (see below for rules). Toddlers may use toy tools and imitate the movements used for tools, but they are not ready for tool use. Preschoolers, on the other hand, have enough motor control and coordination to use tools. They can also focus a little better to stay on task. Before using tools, you should go over some safety basics with children (and other coteachers) and then have an adult supervise them. The amount of supervision will depend on the abilities of the children. Younger preschoolers will probably need an adult to help them hold a tool correctly. As they get more experienced and gain more coordination, they will do more things on their own. Schoolagers will need supervision as well, and the amount will vary widely because some will have no experience with tools and others will have quite a bit.

You can also create a take-apart area and use tools to take apart appliances (Slack and Martin 2015). You don't need a workbench, just a few screwdrivers and goggles. There is no need for clamps or vices. As noted earlier, be sure to open the appliance first to remove any power source (cut cords, remove batteries), transformers, and resistors.

Basic Rules for Tools

1. Tools are not toys. A tool has one use and should be used only for that reason, as opposed to toys, which are made to be used in many ways.
2. Goggles should be worn when using tools. This not only protects children but can also help remind them that they need to focus on the workbench. You can also limit the number of children at the workbench based on the number of goggles, especially if you are using hammers and saws, which require quite a bit of room.
3. Tools should be used only at the workbench (or designated tool area). This helps adults supervise the use of tools and reminds children to respect the tools. They can be dangerous if not used correctly.

Woodworking Tools and Materials

Wood is the main material used by children. It is rigid, yet it can be cut fairly easily with hand tools. Soft woods, such as white pine, cedar, fir, and redwood, are the easiest to use since children are using hand tools. Cardboard also works well for schoolagers, but it bends too easily for younger children to have much success. Cardboard requires cutting with utility knives (see below for more on utility knives).

Clamps and vices are important to keep the wood from slipping when children are using tools. It is hard for preschoolers to keep track of one hand holding the wood while the other hand is using the tool. Clamps allow them to focus on using the tool. C clamps or other clamps that tighten by screwing and unscrewing are preferable to wood clamps that use springs (think of giant metal clothespins). Vices attach to the table and then have separate jaws that hold the wood.

Hammers are often the first tool children like to use because they mostly rely on power and some control, which develop first in children. This gives children a sense of accomplishment as they watch nails go into wood. You can also use hammers to open walnuts and other hard natural materials. Hammers come in different weights. I find that ten-ounce hammers usually work well for preschoolers and sixteen-ounce hammers for schoolagers, although that will depend on the experience and strength of the children, of course. Remember, the lighter the hammer, the more force the child has to use.

Nails are pounded in with a hammer. You want to make sure that the nails are shorter than the depth of the wood you are using so the points don't stick out the other side. You can teach the children to hold the nail on the edge of the wood to see whether it is too long. Roofing nails and common nails have larger heads, so they are good ones to start with. You may want to start nails for younger children, showing them how to use short strokes to get the point into the wood. Once the nail can stand by itself, you can use a longer stroke. You can also poke the nail through a piece of paperboard or hold it with a comb so your fingers aren't in the way. I find that this is harder for young children than holding it themselves. If they are using small strokes with the hammer, the risk of injury is minimal. They may hit their finger or thumb, and they may cry a bit, but they are usually fine after a minute. In my experience, a child learns in a matter of minutes how to avoid hitting their finger again. When children are learning to hammer, the nails will get bent fairly often. If that happens, you simply use the claw end of the hammer to pull the nail out.

Screws are also used to hold wood together. They are similar to bolts, but they have a point that bores into the wood. Drywall screws work well for soft woods. You can also use wood screws. As with nails, make sure the screw is shorter than the depth of the wood. The screws should have a Phillips head, which looks like a plus sign. You can get screws with other heads, but they will require other types of screwdrivers. You will need to drill a pilot hole into the wood to start the screw. A pilot hole is a small hole just narrower than the screw. For soft wood, the hole just needs to be deep enough that the pointy end of the screw fits in.

Screwdrivers require a slight downward force while also requiring rotation. It is easier to unscrew something than screw it in, so young children may have more fun taking things apart. Many electronic appliances can be taken apart. Older electronics have more to unscrew. You may need several sizes of screwdrivers (almost all screws will have Phillips heads). You may find some flat-head screws as well, which just look like a straight line.

It is important to disconnect the power supply of the appliance you are taking apart. Cut the power cord and take out batteries. You may also need to discharge the capacitors in the unlikely event that one is holding a charge. This is especially true of televisions and microwave ovens. You can do this by touching the metal leads of the capacitors with an insulated screwdriver.

Saws take a bit of coordination to use, so I find older preschoolers do better sawing wood that is only about one inch thick, such as one-by-twos and one-by-threes. If we have to cut two-by-fours for something we are building, I will often precut about halfway. Otherwise, I find kids give up before completing a cut. You should use a miter box to hold the wood in place while sawing. Young children often try to saw quickly with short strokes, but it is better to slow down and use the whole length of the blade. If the saw gets stuck, it means too much pressure is being applied. You have to lift the saw up a bit and move slowly. Sawing also requires measuring, so it would be good to have a tape measure or ruler. Schoolagers may be able to do the measuring themselves, but you should remind them to measure twice and cut once. Even adults make mistakes.

Drills require a lot more hand coordination, and it can be difficult to find a non-motorized hand drill, but they are very useful. The drill requires a downward force with one hand while turning the crank with the other. I often have to help children apply the downward force because they tend to tilt the drill. Many schoolagers will be able to use an electric hand drill (or screw gun) if their hands are big enough to reach the trigger. For either type of drill, it is important to have sharp bits so the child doesn't have to apply too much force (i.e., let the bit do the cutting).

Wrenches are used to tighten nuts and bolts. Young children can use adjustable wrenches for a variety of nuts, but not locking pliers (see note under pliers). You can also use socket wrenches, but be sure to keep track of all the pieces. You can also have a variety of wrenches and make sure the nuts fit.

Pliers can be used to twist wire or bend malleable materials. Older preschoolers usually have enough coordination to use pliers, but it depends on how the pliers fit in the child's hand. Children under the age of seven should not use locking pliers (vice grips) because they often have a hard time keeping track of where their fingers of one hand are while the other hand is using the tool.

Utility knives can be used by children around the age of ten. Obviously they still need adult supervision. Utility knives are great for cutting cardboard. Cardboard pieces can then be attached with a staple gun, tape, or papier-mâché.

Staple guns can be used for attaching cardboard. Plier staplers (think heavy-duty stapler) can attach pieces of cardboard to each other. Regular staple guns can attach cardboard to wood. Children should be around the age of ten before using staple guns, because they take a lot of strength to use.

Rethinking Interest Areas

Rethinking interest areas isn't just about children moving; it's about them becoming more actively engaged. When children are moving their bodies, they are more likely to focus their attention on the activity. I have found that as the children in my care gained more freedom in their movement, they became more persistent and independent. I actually had to intervene less. The ideas listed above will hopefully help you in the same way. I realize you probably already do some of these things, and you may not want to try other ideas. The important thing to remember is that you will always be making some changes as children's interests ebb and flow. If an interest area seems to get ignored or causes a lot of conflict, you can ask yourself these questions:

What do I want children to experience/learn?

What will help them with these goals?

How can I accommodate boisterous children? Quieter children? Children with a variety of physical and behavioral needs?

Children are born moving, and they continue to move. Our role as teachers is to channel that energy in ways that encourage discovery, collaboration with others, and active learning. The learning environment plays a major part in this by fostering independence and interdependence among the children. This frees you up to have deeper conversations with individual children. Teaching with the body in mind doesn't mean we teach less—it means children can learn more.

Moving Forward

I have talked quite a bit about encouraging children to explore and to express themselves to foster courage and confidence in them. But it is just as important that we have the confidence and courage to speak out for children. The restrictions on movement imposed on young children have been accompanied by a focus on academics in the interest of school readiness.

True learning happens when the body and mind work together. The reliance on standardized tests to measure progress—tests that require children to sit still for long periods of time—is only one of many hurdles to overcome. We are expecting children to sit for longer and longer periods of time. The current trend of universal pre-K in the United States is wonderful in that all children (or at least four-year-olds) could have access to early childhood education. However, these schools must be "child-ready" and not squelch children's curiosity and energy. We need universal exploration and universal expression for all children. These changes will require many of us to speak up and to find new ways to prepare future teachers.

Before we can do this, *we* need to change as teachers. I have found that the changes I have incorporated have made my teaching easier *and* more effective. I enjoy teaching more, and I am constantly amazed at the abilities of my students. And the more I talk about these changes—the ones put forth in this book—the more I meet other teachers who have made similar discoveries. I have talked to many family child care providers who have been in the field for decades, who have always taught this way but have felt less and less confident about their teaching. As they open up, I find that my "revelations" have been the teaching practices for many for a long time. Meanwhile the accepted practices of our field as a whole and the society at large have made too many of us ignore the children in front of us.

We need to embrace childhood. The children who just won't sit still are reminding us that all children should be moving. We have chosen to ignore this and instead tried to change them. We want them to be more like us. Adults have chosen lifestyles that are frequently sedentary, much to the detriment of our own health. Our society is starting to recognize that adults need to get up and move around. Maybe instead of trying to make the children more like us, we need to be more like them.

References

Almon, Joan. 2013. *Adventure: The Value of Risk in Children's Play*. Annapolis, MD: Alliance for Childhood.

Ball, David, Tim Gill, and Bernard Spiegal. 2012. *Managing Risk in Play Provision: Implementation Guide*. 2nd ed. London: National Children's Bureau.

Bedard, Tom. 2015. *Sand and Water Tables* (blog). www.tomsensori.blogspot.com.

Brannigan, Christopher R., and David A. Humphries. 1972. "Human Non-Verbal Behaviour, a Means of Communication." In *Ethological Studies of Child Behaviour*, edited by N. Blurton Jones, 37–64. London: Cambridge University Press.

Carlson, Frances M. 2006. *Essential Touch: Meeting the Needs of Young Children*. Washington, DC: National Association for the Education of Young Children.

———. 2011a. *Big Body Play: Why Boisterous, Vigorous, and Very Physical Play Is Essential to Children's Development and Learning*. Washington, DC: National Association for the Education of Young Children.

———. 2011b. "Rough Play: One of the Most Challenging Behaviors." *Young Children* 66 (4): 18–25.

Centers for Disease Control and Prevention. 2014. "Nonfatal Injury Reports, 2001–2014." http://webappa.cdc.gov/sasweb/ncipc/nfirates2001.html.

Connell, Gill, and Cheryl McCarthy. 2014. *A Moving Child Is a Learning Child: How the Body Teaches the Brain to Think (Birth to Age 7)*. Minneapolis, MN: Free Spirit Publishing.

DeBenedet, Anthony T., and Lawrence J. Cohen. 2010. *The Art of Roughhousing: Good Old-Fashioned Horseplay and Why Every Kid Needs It*. Philadelphia: Quirk Books.

Epstein, Ann S. 2014. *The Intentional Teacher: Choosing the Best Strategies for Young Children's Learning*. Rev. ed. Washington, DC: National Association for the Education of Young Children.

Evans, Betsy. 2016. *You Can't Come to My Birthday Party!: Conflict Resolution with Young Children*. 2nd ed. Ypsilanti, MI: HighScope Press.

Froschl, Merle, and Barbara Sprung. 2008. "A Positive and Pro-active Response to Young Boys in the Classroom." *Exchange*, 182:34–36.

Gagen, Linda M., Nancy Getchell, and Greg Payne. 2009. "Motor Development in Young Children: Implications and Applications." In *Informing Our Practice: Useful Research on Young Children's Development*, edited by Eva L. Essa and Melissa M. Burnham, 145–61. Washington, DC: National Association for the Education of Young Children.

Galinsky, Ellen. 2010. *Mind in the Making: The Seven Essential Skills Every Child Needs*. New York: Harper.

Gartrell, Dan. 2012. Education for a Civil Society: How Guidance Teaches Young Children Democratic Life Skills. Washington, DC: National Association for the Education of Young Children.

Gilliam, Walter S. 2005. *Prekindergarteners Left Behind: Expulsion Rates in State Prekindergarten Programs*. New York: Foundation for Child Development.

Head Start Bureau. 2004. *Building Blocks for Father Involvement. Building Block 2: First Thoughts on Getting Fathers Involved in Head Start*. Arlington, VA: Head Start Bureau.

Jones, N. Blurton. 1972. "Categories of Child-Child Interaction." In *Ethological Studies of Child Behaviour*, edited by N. Blurton Jones, 97–128. London: Cambridge University Press.

Knight, Sara. 2011. "Why Adventure and Why Risk in the Early Years?" *ChildLinks*, 3:15–18.

Levin, Diane E., and Nancy Carlsson-Paige. 2006. *The War Play Dilemma: What Every Parent and Teacher Needs to Know*. 2nd ed. New York: Teachers College Press.

Marion, Marian. 2014. "Reflecting on Rules and Making Room for Messy Play." In *The Power of Emergent Curriculum: Stories from Early Childhood Settings* by Carol Anne Wien, 48–49. Washington, DC: National Association for the Education of Young Children.

Morhard, Ruth Hanford. 2013. *Wired to Move: Facts and Strategies for Nurturing Boys in an Early Childhood Setting*. Lewisville, NC: Gryphon House.

National Program for Playground Safety. 2015. "Injuries." Accessed July 15. http://playgroundsafety.org/research/injuries.

Nelson, Bryan G. 2002. *The Importance of Men Teachers: And Reasons Why There Are So Few. A Survey of Members of NAEYC*. Minneapolis: Men Teach.

Porter, Rick. 1994. "Roughhousing as a Style of Play." *Exchange*, no. 5: 44–45.

Post, Jacalyn, and Mary Hohmann. 2011. *Tender Care and Early Learning:*

Supporting Infants and Toddlers in Child Care Settings, 2nd ed. Ypsilanti, MI: HighScope Press.

Ratey, John J. 2008. *Spark: The Revolutionary New Science of Exercise and the Brain*. New York: Little, Brown.

Sandseter, Ellen Beate Hansen. 2013. "Early Childhood Education and Care Practitioners' Perceptions of Children's Risky Play: Examining the Influence of Personality and Gender." *Early Child Development and Care* 184 (3): 434–49.

Shumaker, Heather. 2012. *It's OK Not to Share: And Other Renegade Rules for Raising Competent and Compassionate Kids*. New York: Tarcher/Penguin.

Slack, Sandra, and Gerin Martin. 2015. *Make Room for Boys!: Helping Boys Thrive in Preschool*. Ypsilanti, MI: HighScope Press.

Smith, Peter K., and Kevin Connolly. 1972. "Patterns of Play and Social Interaction in Pre-school Children." In *Ethological Studies of Child Behaviour*, edited by N. Blurton Jones, 65–96. London: Cambridge University Press.

Smith-Bonahue, Tina, Sondra Smith-Adcock, and Jennifer Harman Ehrentraut. 2015. "'I Won't Be Your Friend If You Don't!': Preventing and Responding to Relational Aggression in Preschool Classrooms." *Young Children* 70 (1): 76–83.

Tannock, Michelle. 2011. "Observing Young Children's Rough-and-Tumble Play." *Australasian Journal of Early Childhood* 36 (2): 13–20.

Thorne, Barrie. 1993. *Gender Play: Girls and Boys in School*. New Brunswick, NJ: Rutgers University Press.

Tinsworth, Deborah K., and Joyce E. McDonald. 2001. *Special Study: Injuries and Deaths Associated with Children's Playground Equipment*. Washington DC: Consumer Product Safety Commission. www.cpsc.gov/PageFiles/108601/playgrnd.pdf.

Willoughby, Marie. 2011. "The Value of Providing for Risky Play in Early Childhood Settings." *ChildLinks*, 3:7–10.

Index

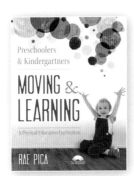
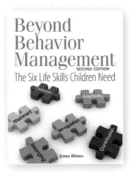

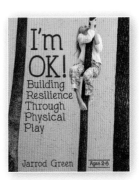